THE CORRUPTORS

BY Nicky Cruz

Satan on the Loose
The Corruptors

THE CORRUPTORS

NICKY CRUZ

16323

FLEMING H. REVELL COMPANY
Old Tappan, New Jersey

Scripture quotations not otherwise identified are from the King James Version of the Bible.

Scripture quotations indentified LB are from The Living Bible. Copyright © 1971 by Tyndale House Publishers, Wheaton, Illinois 60187.

Scripture quotations identified PHILLIPS are from The New Testament in Modern English translated by J. B. Phillips, copyright J. B. Phillips, 1958, 1960, 1972. Used by permission of the Macmillan Publishing Co., Inc.

New Testament Scripture quotations identified TEV are from the Today's English Version of the New Testament. Copyright © American Bible Society, 1966, 1971.

Proverbs Scripture quotation identified TEV is from Wisdom for Modern Man: Proverbs and Ecclesiastes in Today's English Version. Copyright © American Bible Society, 1972.

Excerpt by Upton Sinclair is reprinted by permission of Hawthorn Books, Inc. from THE CUP OF FURY by Upton Sinclair. Copyright © 1956 by Upton Sinclair. All rights reserved.

Excerpt by Jack London is reprinted by permission of Hawthorn Books, Inc. from JOHN BARLEYCORN by Jack London. All rights reserved.

Excerpt from interview with Roberta Blankenship is reprinted by permission from CAMPUS LIFE Magazine, January 1973, © 1973, Youth for Christ, Wheaton, Illinois.

Excerpts from "An 18-Year-Old Looks Back on Life," copyright © 1972 by Joyce Maynard published in LOOKING BACK by Joyce Maynard. Reprinted by permission of Doubleday & Company, Inc.

Some special identifications in this book have been altered or disguised to protect the privacy of the individuals involved.

Library of Congress Cataloging in Publication Data

Cruz, Nicky.
    The corruptors.

    1. Christian life—1960–   2. Civilization,
Modern—1950–   I. Title.
BV4501.2.C78   248'.4   74-12104
ISBN 0-8007-0684-6

TO my dearest friends Becky and Hugh Cummings
who are beautiful Christian people.
They have been more than friends.
They have been like parents.

ACKNOWLEDGMENTS

Jeanie and Kirk Weyant

LaRue Price—my personal secretary who spent many long
hours and much overtime in writing and reviewing, working directly with the publishers, and sacrificing time with
her children during the past several months

Dear wife, Gloria, who has helped me so much and worked
very closely with me.

Contents

Introduction

You may get mad at what I say in this book. Well, I didn't write it to make friends. I didn't write it to make enemies, either. I wrote it because I had to.

It started out a completely different book. But in the last year the world has changed so much. And I've changed. When Jesus spoke to me in a hotel room in Ottawa, Canada, what a difference it made in my life.

Now I see everything with new eyes.

Everywhere you look these days there is corruption and destruction. There are powers loose in the world that are out to get us. If you don't want them to destroy you and yours, let me show you what God has shown me.

Meet the *Corruptors.*

THE CORRUPTORS

1

Crash!

One of the fabulous stars of the entertainment world was Janis Joplin. She didn't just sing. When she got on a stage she was a whirling dervish in perpetual motion, twisting and rocking and shimmying until her gyrations and her lusty voice and the beat all blurred into one wild call to abandon. Janis's fans blew their minds. So many of them swarmed to see her sing and buy her records that all over the rock world Janis Joplin was queen of the scene.

It wasn't always so. As a teen-ager Janis felt fat and pimply and ugly. While she was in school, someone called her Ugliest Man on Campus. But then she learned to give the rock hounds what they wanted. Some people say she chased girls as well as men, tried all kinds of drugs and sex. Onstage she struck one listener like a lonely little girl telling dirty jokes. Offstage, she got deeper and deeper into trouble.

Janis Joplin soared clear to the top of the rock world. Then one night, after two drinks of vodka with friends, she shot some heroin in her hotel room. Returning to the lobby to purchase some cigarettes, she fell as she stepped back into her room, breaking her nose as she died. She was twenty-seven years old. Records show official cause of death as an accidental overdose of heroin.

Janis Joplin wanted desperately to reach the top of her world. She made it! But as she climbed onto her throne, her suicidal life-style brought her whole kingdom crashing down in a tragic end. *It took just five years to travel from superstar to death.*

You can spend your whole life searching for an impossible dream—you may even find it—and you can miss everything important. While I was in a city in the Southwest, a man in cowboy boots and a rancher's hat came to see me. "All my life I've wanted to do something worthwhile," he sobbed, "and now the years are running out and what have I got to show for it? A herd of range cattle not worth the land they graze on!" That rancher knew he had missed out on the most important things there are.

In the summer of 1973 Theodore and Jean Gilbert were having lunch in the New York hotel where they rented an apartment when there was a sound like an explosion. Jean put down her chicken sandwich and Theodore looked out into the hallway and gulped. The hall was gone. Outside the apartment door there was nothing but smoggy sky.

"Hey, Baby," shouted Theodore, "the building just fell down!"

Before it collapsed, the Broadway Central Hotel had been one of New York's finest buildings. For over a hundred years it had stood proud and tall, eight stories high, housing six theaters and more than three hundred tenants. It had been a landmark moldy with history. There Diamond Jim Brady had flashed his famous jewelry; there James Fisk, the railroad tycoon, was shot in a love triangle. There in recent years New York City housed many of its welfare patients, and drug addicts had sometimes roamed the halls.

Now, in a moment, the hotel's floors buckled, the walls ballooned out, the timbers popped and snapped, and in seconds three-fourths of the building collapsed like a house built with matchsticks. Fortunately, before the rest of the hotel fell into the basement, firemen arrived with cherry pickers and scooped the Gilberts and other tenants to safety. Then the remaining rooms and timbers shuddered and tore loose and crashed down into what was now only a heap of rubble. Some of the tenants were buried there. In the final collapse a baby was blown out of its carriage by the blast. The survivors called it a kaleidoscope of terror.

So, in barely the time it takes to read about it, the Broadway Central Hotel with its century of memories collapsed into a heap of bricks, wood, plaster, furniture, metal, glass, bodies, and dust. The whole thing was a kind of modern parable. The Broadway Central went from glory to disaster. The people in it at different times had really lived—they thought! There they had some of the highest experiences and greatest pleasures possible, and some of the lowest and worst. As the hotel neared its end, its imposing appearance was no more than that—a shell covering realities too weak to last. When the end arrived, everything collapsed into nothing.

Only a few years ago the world looked so good. Many kinds of diseases had been wiped out and people were living longer than ever before. The standard of living was rising; there were plans to wipe out poverty. Humans had explored the earth and were starting in on the moon and stars.

Today a lot of people are hungry and some are starving. The human life-span may be getting shorter again. We're running out of living space and food and fuel. There seems to be a shortage these days of nearly everything. The fight against inflation and pollution looks about lost. We are being shocked senseless by criminality in business, in labor, in the armed forces, in government—in everything. America used to tell other countries how to be like us. Now we're scrambling to get ourselves through the rest of the twentieth century.

No, it wasn't long ago that man thought he had conquered nature, space, the atom, the mysteries of the mind and the universe—everything but sin! Today how different everything is. Today's problems are hunger, shortages, pollution, violence, criminality, greed, chaos!

Whether it's the world, or the nation, or a life, everything can come crashing down to sudden destruction. I don't want to see it happen to anyone. So let's look at some of the causes.

Why did the Broadway Central Hotel collapse? The people who lived there said the walls shook every time a subway train went past. Fire Chief John O'Hagan said that the subways and the traffic in the streets weakened the building with their vibrations until it couldn't stand anymore and fell apart.

Isn't that what killed Janis Joplin? Bad vibrations that hit her again and again until she couldn't stand anymore and her life collapsed? Isn't that what's wrong with a lot of people today—and the world?

I know this—you can get so used to bad vibrations that you don't notice them. The people at the Broadway Central got so they hardly ever thought about it when a subway rumbled past. But everything takes its toll, whether you're aware or not, and the end can come mighty fast.

Today, when everything seems touched in some way by corruption, I can see the bad vibrations reaching into every corner of existence. It's going to take a lot of strength and stamina for anyone to *stand* when so much is shaking loose and falling apart.

But you can do it! I know that because I've felt the bad vibrations so often in my own experience, and I've learned how to survive. Here's what I've found out.

2

What Do You Put
in Your Head?

A woman who opened her home to a number of foster-children had trouble with one of them over a certain movie. Ann insisted on seeing it. "Everyone else is going to see it," she said. "Why can't I?"

At the time, the woman was making Jell-O. "Ann," she asked, "Where's the garbage from the lunch dishes?"

"Under the sink. Why?"

"Because I want to use it. Please dump the garbage in the Jell-O."

"The *garbage*? It will spoil it! What do you want to put it in the Jell-O for?"

"If the garbage spoils it," said the foster-mother, "I can always throw the Jell-O out. But if you fill your head with garbage like that movie, I can't throw out your head."

A little later Ann turned down a friend's invitation to go with her to the movie in question. "My parents," she said proudly, "are very strict about what I see. Besides, why should I fill my head with that garbage?"

It's true. More garbage is being distributed today, in movie theaters and books and on TV and newsstands, than ever before in history. But if you think I'm going to say that you should never go to a movie, you're wrong. I know some fine Christian people who never go, and I admire them for their stand. They are saving themselves from a mental diet of garbage! However, I admit that there are some motion pictures I like. I know young people who were brought to Christ by seeing *The Cross and the Switchblade* and have met men and women who were inspired by the play or movie, *A Man for All Seasons.*

Even so, one fact we have to face is this: pornographic magazines, films, and shows make up one of the biggest business operations in the world today. In one recent year 200 million dollars worth of such smut was sold in America. In spite of governmental efforts to put some kind of lid on this dirty business, illicit sex seems to be a surefire success formula for the worst kinds of articles, books, and movies.

One of today's best-selling novelists writes such amateurish fiction that it would be hard to imagine anyone plowing through her books except for the sex that drips from nearly every page. Someone called this author's first novel a "candy box of vulgarity." Filled with sex perversion, drinking, and drug addiction, the book naturally became a popular movie. A magazine editor invited to watch the filming said about her visit to the movie set, "I heard more four-letter words in ten days on that set than I heard in four years at Sarah Lawrence."

The woods are full of people exploiting sex for money.

Books and magazines, movies, and even television shows seem to be built more and more often around sex and violence. One book claimed that it described more than a thousand seductions. Another advised young women on how to trap married men. Other books are billed as sex-filled, sadistic and orgiastic. A reviewer said of one novel, "Color this one dirty. It's been a while since I've seen so much filth outside the barnyard."

Across the nation and in many corners of the world, newsstands are filled with books and magazines that seem to have little to offer except large quantities of sex and nudity. Some of these are so vilely sadistic and pornographic that it is hard to understand how human beings can even prepare and distribute such literature.

But the pornography pushers are not all in the publishing business. Popular songs, often filled with double meanings, pound ideas about the delights of illicit sex and drugs into unsuspecting minds. All kinds of commercial products are tied to sex symbolism for quick success.

Advertisements are getting more and more suggestive. Travel ads promise that girls in bikinis will surround you the moment you arrive. An ad for alcohol pictures a blonde leaning back, glass in hand, and promises that if you mix her a Flaming Flimflam, "you might really stir up something." An ad for a bus line shows a couple snuggling close and suggests that if you go by Flatfoot Bus, "You'll make out better." A shaving cream company uses burlesque music as background for a shapely blonde's cry, "Take it off, take it all off!"—while an actor shaves off his stubble. There is bedtime perfume, and perfume that "makes things happen. What kind of things? That's her affair." For the men, there is an advertisement showing a girl about to get out of a well-used bed asking herself whether it was him, or his cologne. There is even one ad for "a topless car."

Remember, every time you buy a book, a magazine or a movie ticket that glorifies the world of smut, you're supporting the *smut business*. Boycott it by refusing to let your money be used to fill the pockets of the porn-producers.

Suppose the book or the magazine or the movie turns out differently from what you expected? You have a perfect right to walk out of the movie and demand your money back. Or to return the book or magazine.

Some people won't admit that this kind of thing is garbage. Or if they do, they may argue that what you read or see can't hurt you.

It can.

Do you remember Charles Manson? He and his friends were convicted of plotting some of the goriest murders in history, including Sharon Tate, the actress, and her friends. Charlie was fascinated by movies. While he and his gang lived on the Spahn Movie Ranch in southern California they made various motion pictures of their own. One was a pornographic movie in which, according to police, Manson used a machete to hack someone's arm. Another film was made of a group orgy celebrating the "initiation" of a fifteen-year-old girl. One of the girls involved said, "The whole scene was perversion like I've never seen before."

One of Manson's pals was Robert Beausoleil, who had played the part of Lucifer in an occult film called *Lucifer Rising*. At the time, Beausoleil has said, he believed he *was* the devil.

Sharon Tate, who was eventually murdered by Manson's friends, appeared in a number of occult movies. Her first major role was in the film *13* or *Eye of the Devil*. The technical adviser was a magician and occult leader who claimed he initiated Miss Tate into witchcraft during the filming of *13*. She played the part of a vampire in the movie *The Fearless Vampire Killers*.

Another actor in *The Fearless Vampire Killers* was the film's writer and director, Roman Polanski, who made a career of weird movies. He wrote the scenario for *Do You Like Women?*, a film about cannibals in Paris who cook and eat pretty young women. Polanski directed *Repulsion,* about a lovely manicurist who gets hallucinations and beats two of her men friends to death. Polanski also wrote and directed the screen version of *Rosemary's Baby,* a film about witchcraft. A consultant for this film was the notorious Satanist, Anton La Vey, who played the devil. After the film was finished, Sharon Tate married Roman Polanski.

In the summer of 1969 Charles Manson's followers crept into the Polanski home and stabbed Sharon Tate and four other people. Before they died, one of the victims asked one of the murderers, "Who are you?"

"I'm the devil," he answered.

A lot of people wondered why Manson's gang committed those horrible murders. I say *you are what you think about.* It wasn't a long step from all those movies about sex and the occult to that bloody death scene in Sharon Tate's bedroom.

In the past, movie stars took pride in their careers. Actors like Gregory Peck, Cary Grant, Gary Cooper, John Wayne, Spencer Tracy, Sidney Poitier, Jane Wyman, Bette Davis, Katharine Hepburn, Janet Leigh and Kathryn Grayson worked hard and long to create real drama and entertainment. Not so today! Now, often the first thing a would-be actor or actress is asked to do in an audition is to take off his clothes. All you seem to need is a good body.

So often that's true in music too. Some rock performances are nothing but invitations to lust. And a lot of modern music—like a lot of movies, television, radio, books and magazines—has become a giant propaganda campaign for drugs, adultery, and demonism. The music of the Beatles and the Rolling Stones helped glorify marijuana and hard drugs. George Harrison, John Lennon, Donovan, the Rolling Stones, Mia Farrow, and Shirley MacLaine created worldwide publicity for the Maharishi Mahesh Yogi. One rock group got so much press coverage that one of the performers said, "I don't see why they would take four mugs like us, who believe in fornication in the streets, and give us all that ink."

And the Rolling Stones have turned out songs with titles like "Let's Spend the Night Together," "Sympathy for the Devil," and "Their Satanic Majesty's Request."

The devil wants to take over your head. Is that what you want?

3

Violence Incorporated

When I was in the gangs in New York, blood and torture, fights and terror were my daily diet. After God reached down through David Wilkerson and lifted me up out of that way of life, I got a jolt when I learned how much violence there was *outside* the ghettos.

The last fourteen years have been a Roman circus of beatings, bombings, tortures, kidnappings, assassinations, massacres, and incredible crimes. Practically every year there has been a dramatic increase in burglaries, robberies, assault, rape, and general law-breaking. The number of crimes in America has more than doubled since 1960—and the sad fact is that most crimes are never reported.

Recently the young grandson of the billionaire J. Paul Getty was kidnapped and held for three million dollars ransom. When the family refused to pay, the kidnappers cut off the boy's ear. He was released when the ransom was put in the extortioners' hands. There seems to be no limit to the wickedness in the world today.

And inhumanity hasn't been cornered by gangsters and loners. Dozens of governments today condone torture to suppress dissent and get information. In Turkey, in Vietnam, and in many other places prisoners have been half-drowned, beaten to the point of

death, and tortured with electrical shocks by intelligence experts
—all in the name of freedom, security, law and order.

One thing I've noticed about the last fourteen years while crime
was increasing so rapidly has been the increase in movies and
TV programs, as well as books and articles in magazines, saturated
with violence. Many people have said there was no connection
between the two. I think they're dead wrong.

How can anyone fill his mind with beatings and killings and
crimes of all kinds and not be affected by it? After Robert Ken-
nedy was assassinated, a National Commission on the Causes and
Prevention of Violence was formed. The commission made a
lengthy study of violence and concluded that violence on TV
encourages violence in the streets. It recommended less program-
ming of violence, removal of violence from children's cartoon
shows, scheduling of crime shows only late in the evening, and
provision for attractive substitutes for the usual TV fare. That
makes a lot of sense.

I can't forget that it was soon after a TV station in Boston
broadcast a show about some teen-agers who set fire to an old
man, that several young people in that city surrounded a woman,
poured gasoline over her, and set her afire. She died after hours
of horrible suffering.

I'm not saying there's anything wrong with TV newscasts. I'm
saying TV should be controlled by parents in the home. Certain
programs should be off limits for children. Each father and
mother should know what their children can or cannot take. TV
serves a very good purpose in educating us on what is happening
in the world today. But like everything else, it can be used or
abused—it can inform or corrupt.

Sometimes when a rock group comes to town it's a signal for
lust and violence to break loose. Because of that some people
blame modern young people for today's violence. Don't think
they are the main cause. Most of the blood-and-thunder-and-sex
films and TV programs are produced not by young people but by
supposedly mature men and women who make their living that

way. I know from experience that some of these porn and violence merchants are "fine" people who live in excellent neighborhoods, belong to respectable organizations, support worthy charities, and raise "nice" families. And if you've ever seen the people buying tickets to a blue movie, you've noticed that many of them aren't young at all, but middle-aged and older. No, in the selling of sex and violence, no one age group has cornered the market. It reaches every part of our society. And it's a problem for all of us.

But I'm not thinking just of the things that make newspaper headlines. The spirit of violence is also the spirit of not caring when someone is in trouble. I think of all the older people suffering in dignified misery—I'll come back to them later. I think of all the people today without jobs and of the children and young people who tell me their parents don't seem to know they exist. I think of the people starving, as I write this, in Africa and Pakistan.

When we hear the morning newscast of things like this, do we *care*? Or do we just reach for another cup of coffee and forget those people are there?

The only real solution to any of our modern problems is to begin where they begin: inside. God knew what He was talking about when He said: "Keep thy heart with all diligence; for out of it are the issues of life" (Proverbs 4:23). Keep your heart warm and sensitive to human need. Keep it sound and straight and uncorrupted, and you've made a good start toward beginning to turn society right side up again.

So listen to what He says in the words of the Apostle Paul:

> Fix your thoughts on what is true and good and right. Think about things that are pure and lovely, and dwell on the fine, good things in others. Think about all you can praise God for and be glad about . . . . and the God of peace will be with you.
>
> Philippians 4:8, 9 LB

Instead of wasting your time on entertainment that leads straight downhill, read some of the great Christian books you can find these days in so many bookstores. Instead of getting curious about things better left unexplored, be curious about why the world is so twisted up and what God wants you to do about it. Think. Pray. Read the Bible. Get together with your Christian friends. Fill your mind and heart with things you can be glad about! Don't leave any room in your life for the things that tear down and corrupt. Let God make you a showcase of the things He wants to give everyone: peace and harmony and rightness and real joy.

4

The Spirit in the Bottle

One route to joy that millions of people try reminds me of a story Aunt Rosa used to tell. Tía Rosa, as we called her, lived all by herself in a tiny house in Las Piedras, Puerto Rico. But her heart was as big as her house was small. She wasn't really my aunt; all the boys and girls in Las Piedras called her that because she treated us all like members of her family. On hot days Tía Rosa gave us all delicious cookies and a cold fruit drink like lemonade, and told us stories. When I was small and I couldn't think of anything else to do I went over to her place sometimes and grabbed as many cookies as I could hold and listened.

The story I'm thinking of started out with a poor fisherman who always seemed to have bad luck. (My editor tells me this story came out of the *Arabian Nights* originally, but I'll tell about it as I remember it.) Every time this fisherman pulled in his net he got something he didn't want—once even a dead horse. But when he was about ready to give up, his net brought in an old copper bottle tightly corked. He pulled out the cork and thought the bottle was empty until smoke started pouring out, and *Wow!* The smoke collected overhead into the shape of a giant! Then the fisherman realized he had uncorked a spirit.

This spirit was a bad one. He told the poor fisherman, who was standing there shaking, that some bad person had put him in the bottle hundreds of years before, stuck in the cork and thrown him

in the ocean. For the first century or two, the spirit thought of all
the good things he would do for anyone letting him out. But as
more centuries passed and he was still stuck, the spirit got more
and more mad. Finally he decided he would kill the first person
to let him out of his bottle-prison. So the fisherman found he was
in worse luck than ever.

The fisherman thought fast. Then he told this giant spirit,
boiling up into the sky over his head, that he just couldn't believe
such a great being could get into that little bottle. The spirit went
back inside to prove it, and the fisherman put the cork back in
the bottle fast and threw the spirit back into the ocean.

I think of that story when I hear people worrying about drugs.
Drugs are corrupting and destroying so many people today that
it makes me sick to think of it. But the awful thing is that too
many of the people who worry about drugs don't realize that the
worst drug of all is getting into more and more homes, right here
in America—Christian homes, too. It's a spirit that hides in a
bottle and destroys the person who lets it out.

I mean *booze*.

Maybe you're thinking, "What do you mean, the worst drug of
all? Surely you don't mean alcohol is as bad as the other awful
drugs being taken today!" I do. I know what alcohol does. But
this isn't just my own idea. In 1973 a federal commission finished
a million-dollar, two-year study of drugs and reported that Drug
Enemy Number One today is not heroin or marijuana or even
LSD but *alcohol*.

The National Commission on Marijuana and Drug Abuse said
that a lot of the information being given out about drugs today
is so incorrect it should be stopped. And it said that a lot of the
drug education may only stimulate interest in harmful drugs.

That checks with my own information. One father told me of
his thirteen-year-old daughter's report on the drug instruction at
her junior high school. She said, "The teacher told us that everyone in our school had tried some kind of drugs. I know that isn't
true, because I don't even want to try drugs, and I know some of
my friends have never tried drugs either."

That father was angry at his daughter's teacher, and I don't blame him. What a perfect method of tempting young people to try drugs! What boy or girl wants to be in the "inexperienced" minority? It's the same thing with sex. Every so often a school or a teacher somewhere does a little survey of the students' "sex experiences." What young person wants to admit being inexperienced?

The National Commission said the producers of alcohol ought to advertise the *dangers* of drinking, and should not slant their ads toward young people.

How I wish that recommendation were law right now! I'd love to see on every bottle of every alcoholic beverage, on every cocktail list in every restaurant and bar, and in every ad for anything alcoholic, the following warning—accompanied by a big red skull and crossbones:

DANGER

ALCOHOL IS THE MOST DANGEROUS DRUG KNOWN TO MAN. IT TWISTS MINDS. IT IS ADDICTIVE. IT KILLS. USE IT AT YOUR OWN RISK, TO THE MORTAL DANGER OF EVERYONE AROUND YOU.

I'm not going to tell anyone not to drink. It should be enough to point out some things everyone should know about this deadly drug. For one thing, alcohol can be very addictive. The physical risk of addiction to alcohol may be only moderate, but the psychological risk is very high. And it's so deceptive. People claim to drink for relaxation, to get rid of anxiety and tension and to get a feeling of peace and well-being. Before they know it, many drinkers are hooked. Today nine million Americans show all the symptoms of alcoholism, and *many of them don't realize it.*

Alcohol does relax—but it can break down your inhibitions—and moral values. It can also decrease your alertness, reduce your powers of coordination, slow down your thinking processes, and produce drowsiness, dizziness, blurred vision, slurred speech, stupor, nausea—and death. Addiction can reduce your life expectancy by ten years or more.

Like most drugs, it takes larger and larger amounts of alcohol to produce the same effects. Continued excessive use damages the stomach, liver, and brain. It can produce obesity, impotence, delirium tremens, and psychosis. Medical men used to believe that alcohol had some medicinal value. Today most realize it has *none.*

There has been considerable complaint about the amount of money the United States has spent in recent years on welfare, foreign aid, and space exploration. For welfare and space we have been spending about $10 billion a year. But we Americans spend $25 billion a year for booze. And the crime, accidents, and health problems caused by alcoholic misuse cost us countless billions more. Half the accidents in homes are connected with drinking. Many drinkers die every year from fires, falling, shooting accidents, drowning, choking, and freezing to death. Sandy Rogers, the soldier son of Roy and Dale Evans Rogers, tragically choked to death in Germany after his buddies enticed him into an unaccustomed drinking spree.

Heavy drinking lowers a person's resistance to pneumonia and other diseases. Alcohol is a major cause of twenty-eight thousand deaths each year from highway accidents. It is involved in nearly half the arrests, a fifth of the divorces, and a third of the suicides in this country.

Upton Sinclair, the brilliant social crusader and Pulitzer Prize winner, knew a lot of famous people who drank: Jack London, for example, one of the most colorful figures in American history. In his teens he shipped as a sailor to Japan. He panned for gold in the Klondike, became an oyster pirate, newspaper correspondent, and brilliant novelist. In his thirties he wrote his autobiography, entitled *John Barleycorn* because alcohol had played so big a part in his life. (He started drinking when he was five!) But in that book he denied that he was an alcoholic and boasted:

> I was never a drunkard, and I have not reformed . . . . I have
> decided coolly and deliberately that I should continue to do what
> I have been trained to want to do. I will drink—but oh, more skill-

fully, more discreetly than ever before. Never again will I be a peripatetic conflagration.

Jack London kept on drinking, kept on alternating between alcohol-induced euphoria and despair, and killed himself at the age of forty.

In his book *The Cup of Fury* Upton Sinclair tells of dozens of such well-known individuals, who all thought they could handle their liquor, but who became its helpless victims. One, not so famous but with a poignant story, was Sinclair's own father, who left home time and again hopeful and happy—and time after time had to be helped home by his teen-age son because he had become a staggering drunkard. Upton Sinclair lost to alcohol's clutches not only his father but three uncles and many friends—seventy-five in all. No wonder he hated and fought against drink all his life!

Once Sinclair went with a friend on a tour of New York behind the scenes. They went from one famous place to another. They stood offstage as the curtains went up on a famous Broadway play. They went into a bar and talked with a justice of the Supreme Court, a professional burglar, a skilled forger, and a New York politician under indictment for his crimes. They toured the night spots.

The thing that impressed Upton Sinclair about all these places was the number of men and women sitting by themselves, drugged, nearly asleep—"having a good time." Describing that night in *The Cup of Fury*, Sinclair adds:

And I thought how many wonderful things there are in this world, so much to do and so much to learn—and so much of it being lost in exchange for the measly, momentary "warm glow" of whiskey.

All my life I have been able to say that I am "drunk without alcohol." To me this universe is one vast mystery story, fascinating beyond any power of words to tell. If I could have my own way, I would stay here a million years to watch what happens.

I am anxious to know "what is going to happen next." I want to know more about what really happened in the past, and I read history. I am also absorbed by astronomy, and by the amazing discoveries which men are making with the new tools of this science . . . .

And then there is the infinitely small universe which science has discovered in the nucleus of the atom. Apparently there are as many nuclear particles in a drop of water as there are stars in the heavens; and who can guess what may turn up inside a proton? We already have found within the atom the power to destroy a city; any day now we may develop the power to heal the world.

And all my life, I have been "drunk" with the intoxicating wonders of good books. With the right book, the world is yours; it waits by your bedside, at your convenience. You can watch the whole pageant of history. You can enter into and share the experiences of the greatest minds that ever lived on earth. You can, in the words of Tennyson, "dip into the future, far as human eye can see." You can climb to the top of Mount Everest; now for the first time you can go down a mile into the bottom of the sea; you can visit climes hot and cold without discomfort; you can go among strange peoples and marvel at their ways of survival; you can hunt wild beasts or catch great fish; you can fly to the farthest galaxies and penetrate the infinite minuteness of the atomic nucleus; you can go inside your own body; you go to Heaven with the saints and to Hell with Dante.

In a world like this, one does not commit suicide "simply because he could no longer drink enough to give him any pleasure!"

I think Upton Sinclair had a tremendous point. When there are so many fascinating things in God's world to enjoy, so many challenges, so many good causes to strengthen and so many wrongs to help right—who wants to stagger half-conscious and half-dead to an unnecessary grave?

But no one has ever summed up this subject more perfectly than the man who wrote this:

Show me someone who drinks too much, who has to try out fancy drinks, and I will show you someone miserable and sorry for himself, always causing trouble and always complaining. His eyes are bloodshot and he has bruises that could have been avoided. Don't let wine tempt you, even though it is rich red, and you can see yourself in the cup, and it looks so good as you swish it around. The next morning you will feel as if you have been bitten by a poisonous snake. Weird sights will appear before your eyes, and you will not be able to think or speak clearly. You will feel as if you were out on the ocean, seasick, swinging high up in the rigging of a tossing ship. "I must have been hit," you will say; "I must have been beaten up, but I don't remember it. Why can't I wake up? I need another drink."

Proverbs 23:29–35 TEV

One of my Christian friends used to enjoy an occasional glass of wine with his meals. He felt perfectly at liberty to do this, but one day I discovered that he no longer drank. When I asked him about this my friend replied:

"Do you remember my brother Vernon? A few years ago he had a terrible time with alcoholism. He's got it licked now, but for his sake I've given up wine. I don't want to do anything that might lead Vernon back into that living hell that tortured him for so long."

There are a lot of Vernons in the world today.

5

This Chemical Age

When one of America's largest chemical manufacturers had a run on a certain poster its promotion department distributed, it was discovered that a lot of copies of this poster were being put on the walls of college students' rooms. The poster said in big letters: BETTER LIVING THROUGH CHEMISTRY.

The students, interested in LSD and other drugs, had a little different idea about the value of chemicals than the manufacturer intended!

But we *do* live in a chemical age. Today it seems like there's a pill for everything. Doctors prescribe pills to pick you up and pills to calm you down. There are drugs to make you happy, drugs to make you relaxed, drugs to help you loose weight and drugs to help you gain.

Sometimes I think that this is the generation that can't wait. When we get up in the morning, we can't wait to get going, so we reach for the coffeepot. If the caffeine in two cups of coffee doesn't stimulate fast enough, some people reach for their pickup pills. When we go to bed, we *have* to get to sleep the minute we turn out the lights. If we don't, we are tempted to reach for the sleeping pills.

This passion for speed is one of today's worst corruptors. Everything has to be instant. People used to be able to wait five or ten minutes to cook breakfast cereal. Now most of it is either "quick" (ready in three or four minutes), or "instant" (ready in seconds), or ready to eat. We demand instant breakfasts, instant potatoes, ready-to-eat dinners and ovens that cook everything quicker than quick. We take courses so that we can read with the "speed of light." We're always trying to shorten the time to get somewhere. Once there, we start figuring the fastest way home. And thousands who travel by plane try to obliterate even these few hours by steeping themselves in alcohol.

We live in a drug society! Drugs of all kinds are becoming more accepted every day. Some of these drugs are legal—and some are not.

One thing that stands out about the entertainment world of today is the amount of drugs in it. Janis Joplin was not the only star wiped out by chemicals. After Marilyn Monroe's sudden death, examination of her blood showed that she may have taken a bottleful of sleeping pills. Apparently barbiturates killed the Beatles' youthful manager, Brian Epstein. A good many rock entertainers have admitted that they rely on various drugs for a good performance. Some composers and writers depend on drugs to get "turned on."

But entertainers and creative people aren't the only ones involved with drugs. How shocked many of us were when Diane, the daughter of my dear friend Art Linkletter, jumped to her death from her fifth-story apartment due to an LSD flashback. That experience led Art to intensive research into the whole drug problem and he has campaigned hard to fight this modern menace.

There is so much misinformation today about drugs! If you doubt that, ask a friend to tell you which of the following is the most dangerous, and which the least:

> **Glue vapor**
> **Amphetamines (stimulants, pep pills)**
> **Alcohol**
> **Cigarettes**
> **Barbiturates and narcotics**
> **Heroin**
> **LSD and related hallucinatory drugs**
> **Marijuana**

Of course, there could be some debate about that. You already know where I rank alcohol, and how the Federal Commission on Drug Abuse rates it. Another expert is Samuel Irvin, professor of psychopharmacology at the Medical School of the University of Oregon. Professor Irvin specializes in studying the effects of drugs on the mind and body. He says that the intrinsic hazard potential is in *the exact order above*. Sniffing glue is the most dangerous, taking amphetamines the second, and so on down the list.

Let's go down the list ourselves.

Sniffing glue is unspeakably dangerous because the sniffer's first whiffs may be his last. Inhaling certain kinds of glue—and certain aerosol sprays—may irreversibly damage a person's lungs and brain, and even cause sudden death. These things should be kept far from anyone not wise enough to avoid experimenting with them.

Amphetamines are stimulants that can supply a quick pickup. They come in the form of benzedrine, dexedrine, pep pills, "speed," and so on, and are highly dangerous because it is so easy to become addicted—psychologically at the very least—and because of what they can do to a person. Although amphetamines are often prescribed for everything from depression to weight control, excessive use can cause hallucinations, convulsions, and even permanent mental disorders. About half the amphetamines get into the underground market, or are manufactured illegally, so they may be contaminated and therefore doubly dangerous.

Alcohol, the inhalants, the barbiturates, the tranquilizers and the narcotics (Demerol, hashish, heroin and other products of the opium poppy) are depressants. They relax—sometimes to the point of stupor, coma, and death. At the other end of the drug scale are the stimulants—the amphetamines, cocaine, synthetic antidepressants, caffeine, and nicotine.

Tobacco, like alcohol, is so widely used that most smokers would be very surprised if you called them drug addicts. But medically speaking, tobacco is indeed a drug, and cigarettes are among the most harmful substances used by man. The evidence has been piling up for years. In 1957 two scientists named Hammond and Horn presented to the American Medical Society a report they had made for the American Cancer Society. Hammond and Horn studied the smoking habits of two hundred thousand men for nearly four years. Their research showed many more deaths and diseases among the smokers than the nonsmokers. The more cigarettes smoked, the more deaths. When the heavy smokers cut down on their cigarettes, fewer of this group died. A very close correlation was found between cigarette smoking and lung cancer.

It was also discovered that the cigarette smokers died much more often than nonsmokers from emphysema, bronchitis, stomach ulcer, heart disease, hypertension, stomach cancer, and other diseases. These statistics held up regardless of the age, height, weight, IQ, location, education, background, or practically any other relationship of the smokers and nonsmokers. The one clear conclusion of all this research was that *cigarettes are one of the surest killers known.*

Similar investigations have been made in other countries. Research in England, Canada and various other nations shows the same relationship between cigarette smoking and all kinds of disease. Great Britain's Royal College of Surgeons has found that smokers may even be more accident-prone than other people. America's Public Health Service studied more than a million smokers and nonsmokers. It found out that the death rate for smokers is 68 percent higher than the incidence for nonsmokers. The rate is 980 percent higher for cancer of the lung, over 500 percent higher for bronchitis and emphysema! That scares me! I hope it scares everyone who reads this book enough so you'll never be addicted to those little white things that used to be jokingly called "coffin nails." Those two words turn out to be about as literal a description as you can find of the legal drug, the sneaky killer—tobacco.

Every time you puff on a cigarette you're taking into your lungs and bloodstream at least *fifteen known poisons and at least seven substances known to cause cancer.* (More poisons and cancer-starters are suspected but not yet completely proven so in laboratory tests.)

Every week a thousand Americans bleed or burn to death or

die in other ways from highway accidents. At least half those deaths are tied to alcohol abuse. Many of them may relate to smoking, since cigarettes decrease night vision. In any case, while cars kill a thousand people a week, cigarettes kill *seven thousand*. That's more deaths than from heroin!

You've heard of the horrible plagues and epidemics of the past —cholera, typhoid, and so on. Would you believe that all those epidemics in Western Europe since the start of the sixteenth century, and all the known epidemics of yellow fever in the history of the world, killed less people than cigarettes kill *every year* in this country? It's true! Please, don't let cigarettes become nails in *your* coffin.

Right here you may be wondering why I haven't said more about drugs like marijuana and LSD and heroin. I wish I had the space! There just isn't room in this book for all I'd like to say about such drugs. Let me mention, though, that David Wilkerson has put together a lot of valuable information about a good many dangerous drugs in his book *Hey, Preach . . . You're Comin' Through!* Read it for some good straight talk on the subject.

Let me just say this about marijuana, since there's so much talk today of legalizing it: **Pot is a corruptor, too.** For many young people, a stick of marijuana is often the first step down the awful trail toward hopeless addiction to the hardest and worst kinds of drugs. And recent medical evidence shows that steady marijuana smokers may become apathetic and confused, and suffer from personality changes and even brain damage.

About heroin, I hope by now everyone knows how dangerous it is. If everyone who has been ruined by heroin could come back from their graves and ghetto holes and speak, what horrible stories they could tell! Maybe such stories are summed up in these words which were found scribbled on a piece of paper in the pocket of a young woman who committed suicide:

King Heroin is my shepherd.
I shall always want.

He maketh me to lie down in the gutters.
He leadeth me beside the troubled waters.
He destroyeth my soul.
He leadeth me in the paths of wickedness.
Yea, I shall walk through the valley of poverty.
I will fear no evil for thou, Heroin, art with me.
Thy Needle and Capsule comfort me.
Thou strippest the table of groceries in the
    presence of my family.
Thou robbest my head of reason.
My cup of sorrow runneth over.
Surely heroin addiction shall stalk me all the
    days of my life, and I will dwell in the
    House of the damned forever.

The girl who wrote that was twenty-three when she killed herself. What a testimony!

It's really depressing to study the effects of practically any of these mind-bending substances. With the depressant drugs the results often are stupor, nausea, blurred vision, a thick tongue, confusion, impotence, unconsciousness, and finally death. With the hallucinogens and the stimulants the effects range from anxiety and panic to irritability, insomnia, delusions, damage to the mind and body, and again, death. It's destruction all the way!

And I'm not at all happy about reports that many young people today are turning away from illicit drugs to legal ones like alcohol. Their parents may be less worried, but the fact is, few people realize how dangerous alcohol and tobacco can be. The important thing to keep in mind is that they are *drugs*.

Let me tell you about Bart, who grew up in a university town in Europe. Through the students he was introduced early to various drugs.

When he was seventeen, Bart had a weird experience. Crossing a field, he suddenly had a vision of the sky splitting open and dropping balls of fire onto the earth, setting fire to everything they touched. Another time, driving along the Baltic coast, he felt that there was going to be an earthquake that would swallow him and everything around him.

Psychiatrists traced these hallucinations to Bart's experiments with drugs. For a time they felt he was schizophrenic, but in recent years, as he has left drugs behind, he has remarkably improved.

Bart said recently: "I don't trust a single thing that can alter the mind. I'm convinced now, from my own experience, that every single drug, including alcohol and pot, is extremely danger- ous. Tell everyone you know, never fool around with your mind."

Yes, the whole drug business, legal or illegal, is one of the monstrous evils of our age. You could call this an age of drugs. Today there's a pill for everything. Doctors prescribe a pill to pick you up and a pill to calm you down. Millions of men and women are hooked on cigarettes and cocktails, on amphetamines to get going in the morning, and barbiturates to get to sleep, and don't even realize it.

Fortunately, many people are concerned about this problem of increasing drug addiction. (Though I don't hear as much alarm about the tendency in so many areas to lower the drinking age.) But how many are asking *why* so many turn to drugs? Why do we so often look at the *surface* of our problems, and so seldom at the real causes?

For one thing, there has been entirely too much publicity that has been more harmful than helpful. It's not enough to tell peo- ple how awful drugs are. They don't scare today any more than their grandparents and great-great-grandparents did when the preachers and temperance lecturers were all denouncing Demon Rum. Describing the awful effects of drugs like heroin and LSD has created a lot of unhealthy curiosity. It reminds me of the mother who told her children as she left them alone in the house, "Don't put any beans in your nose." The children would never have thought of such a thing if their mother hadn't given them the idea. As it was, they kept thinking of her parting words, and before long they found some beans. They had to find out what it felt like to stick beans up their noses, and when the mother got home every last child had beans stuck in his nose!

That's something like today's drug problem. All the publicity about crime and drug addiction and illicit sex and other related evils has led a good many people to try some of them to see what they might have been missing. That may be a stupid reaction, but I'm afraid it's also human nature. What we most need today is not so much more *information*—helpful as some of it may be, when properly presented—as more *desire to serve the Lord and help other people*. That's where every Christian can help.

To understand today's drug scene, let's look at what life was like when I was in the gangs of New York City. I *know* why so many of the gang members took pot and smack. Everyone in the gangs had this terrible feeling of emptiness, loneliness, sadness, and frustration. Drugs gave one kind of security and peace, and sometimes thrills which helped us forget the emptiness inside.

To many of us in the New York gangs, life often looked like one big hoax. We saw the hustlers and pushers driving around in Cadillacs, the cops and judges they paid off, and the decent people living in squalor and fear. We figured the one sure way to get ahead was to grab quickly all you could. It's not easy to see much future in that environment. So grab a reefer or a bottle or a needle and float off for a little while on some rosy cloud of temporary happiness! The tragedy of it all is that the trip is always so short, and you always hit so hard when you come down, and drugs write off your few chances to find anything better in life.

Our whole culture has a big empty spot in the middle. Unless Christ fills that spot, it's going to be filled with some counterfeit saviour.

Do you want to know why I don't need drugs of any kind? Because I've found a way to get everything they can provide, and much more. Would you like more energy, more zest in life, bigger thrills than you ever dreamed possible? One teen-ager who had been hooked on a number of drugs explained why he became interested in Christ. He met some young people from a Christian coffeehouse in New Milford, New Jersey. This is what he said about them:

> See, these kids came along and wanted to rap, and that was okay with me. I didn't mind—I was high on "coke." But five hours later my high was gone, and those kids were still high—on Jesus! Man, I tell you, that made me think. Now I'm all the way into Jesus, because He gives you a high that never lets you down.

But suppose you need a downer. Maybe you're too keyed up and you can't sleep. Don't reach for a sleeping pill. Instead, lie back and just meditate on the wonderful fact that the Lord is your Shepherd and Friend. You can never solve all your problems, but He can. Praise Him for that! Thank Him that He has everything under control. Let truths like that sink into your heart and mind, and you'll find a peace "which is far beyond human understanding," sweeping through your soul (*see* Philippians 4:7 TEV).

Dangerous as drugs are, there are worse problems today. Right now a good many young people are turning away from drugs. Many young people are very intelligent about the mind-benders; they know drugs can blow a mind sky-high. So the use of drugs may be decreasing.

Too many young people are turning instead to witchcraft and the occult.

6

The Occult

I wrote my last book *Satan on the Loose* because it has been impressed on me that one of the most corrupting forces in the world today is the occult. Fascination with this dark side of the supernatural is sweeping through every country and every area of life. Once such interest was limited to five-dollar fortune-tellers in back alleys and to séances in small dark rooms where desperately searching men and women tried to make contact with someone they had lost in death. Not any more! Today the occult is big business. Books, movies, games, schools—everyone seems to be trying to cash in on the tremendous interest in the supernatural.

It's very interesting that so many people who should know better are getting involved in the occult today. For many, God has been booted out the front door—but Satan and witchcraft and all the rest have sneaked in through the back door. On an airplane flight between Tucson and Dallas I sat next to a woman who was reading a book of astrology. When she saw me glance at her book she said, "You look like a Capricorn."

"You're right," I said, "but I have something better than astrology." Then I told her that I don't need to find out what influences the stars may have on my life, for I know the One who holds the stars in the hollow of His hand. This lady looked very uncomfortable as I talked about Jesus. I've found truth so often in what Paul said:

Don't be teamed with those who do not love the Lord, for what do the people of God have in common with people of sin? How can light live with darkness? And what harmony can there be between Christ and the devil?

2 Corinthians 6:14, 15 LB

So many people who feel they are too modern or intelligent to believe in the Bible, accept the most ridiculous things if they have an occult label. The late Bishop James Pike at one time seemed to be a serious Christian thinker. Then he began doubting different things in the Christian faith. At one point he said that he could *sing* the Apostles's Creed but that he could not conscientiously *say* it—because he could no longer accept what it said.

Bishop Pike may have first gotten interested in spiritualism soon after he became an Episcopal priest. He heard strange noises in his parsonage in Poughkeepsie, New York. Candles which he lit were mysteriously extinguished, according to Hans Holzer, and once he collided with a bat. Later, in New York and England, he heard more strange noises and found books and other objects inexplicably moved about behind locked doors.

Bishop Pike gave spiritualism and occultism a tremendous boost when he took part in a television séance with the famous medium, Arthur Ford. Through this and other dealings with mediums here and abroad, the Bishop exposed millions of people to the false claims of this so-called religion which has often been mixed up in all kinds of fakery and deceit. It seems a fitting end to his career that when Bishop Pike was lost in a desert in Israel, his wife contacted various mediums—some of whom said he was alive and well, although it was soon discovered that he was dead.

When Bishop Pike questioned the Trinity he probably felt he was being very modern, but actually I wonder if he was not slipping backward into the worst kinds of superstition. If I have to choose between believing in the Trinity or believing in mediums, I don't want to have to put my trust in mediums.

While I was writing this chapter, a friend brought me an advertisement from a well-known book club. PUT THE POWER OF

THE OCCULT AT YOUR COMMAND! the advertisement says. There follows a magical mixture of books, tarot cards, numerology games, astrology charts, everything imaginable to involve people in the occult. Everywhere things of this kind are coming out into the open. In the streets of Rome and Los Angeles witches march, demanding the right to practice their bestial rites openly. In England and Europe graves are opened, tombstones are broken, churches are desecrated, debasing acts are performed. In America, Satan is worshiped! More and more psychics are winning popular approval. In California a man with allegedly psychic powers, Uri Geller, recently came to Stanford University to try to prove that his powers exist. It is claimed that Uri can read minds, bend keys and snap spoons without touching them, and even repair watches by unknown powers. He says that he does not think such power comes from his mind: "I believe it is generated through me by an intelligent power in the universe. I believe in God, but I do not believe this is coming from God."

If Uri Geller's strange abilities come from some intelligent power in the universe which is not God . . . *what is that power?*

In *Satan on the Loose* I mentioned the forms of the occult that are ensnaring so many people today. I keep hearing of new examples all the time. A bright, attractive college student recently reported her experiences as a witch. Ron Hutchcraft of *Campus Life* interviewed this girl, Roberta Blankenship, and asked what first attracted her to witchcraft. This was her answer:

> The funny thing is, I wasn't really attracted to it. It just sort of happened to me. It began at a junior high school slumber party when someone suggested we try a séance, just for fun. I didn't know how to run one, but I agreed to try. That night I began to realize some unusual power, and I decided to develop it. I started experimenting.

The occult power which Roberta was now contacting appealed to her because she hated her environment and wanted revenge:

> My life at home was very violent. My mother and stepfather were constantly drinking and fighting, and it got pretty physical sometimes. I began to pity myself, and I lapsed into deep depression, resenting my family. I wanted to hurt because I'd been hurt.

The séance led to more:

> My friends and I began to get little signs we were "making contact"—like a knock on the wall or something. Then we started to hear vocal correspondence . . . kids could recognize them as the voices of departed people. On some occasions there were visual formations—not solid figures, but with human features that identified them as male or female faces.
>
> The deeper we got into the occult, the more frightened the other kids became. Many were scared off.

But not Roberta. She enjoyed the strange powers.

> I led groups in the use of levitation and ouija boards. I stressed that we always use the ouija boards without hands to avoid human manipulation. This was no game to me.
>
> Soon I was into astrology and horoscopes. My girlfriends were impressed with these new fields, but I thought people were really being fooled by horoscopes—most were simple common sense and could apply to anyone. After astrology it was palmistry, Tarot cards, and the crystal ball.
>
> During this time I was having psychic visions that foretold the future. I even lost friends when the visions became true—they were getting very frightened of me. They heard me predict things like Robert Kennedy's assassination, my sister being hit by a car and numerous incidents in kids' lives. By that time, the word was really spread around school—Roberta is a witch.

Ron Hutchcraft asked Roberta whether she ever used her powers to hurt someone. Sometimes she did:

> . . . against people who were against me. I found I could cause accidents, illnesses and misfortune for people by using hexes. That is black magic. But I never *told* anyone about the hex—people can get psyched out by that and *cause* it to happen. I did it quietly and then sat back to watch my power work.

Roberta was invited to join a coven of witches, but refused because she felt their witchcraft was weak. The witches ascribed their power to the devil or some other deity; Roberta felt that her power was all her own!

Still, all that power didn't satisfy her. "My messed-up world wasn't changing. My home was still full of hate; I had no close friends. In fact, I attempted suicide."

At home, alone, she picked up a butcher knife to cut her wrists when she envisioned demons shouting with a single voice: "Roberta, you fool. *I* gave you all your powers." The demonic entity declared that Roberta was its slave as long as she lived, that she would not die until it was through with her. On that day Roberta Blankenship promised to worship and serve the devil.

But nothing she did helped make her into the kind of person she wanted to become. She was suspicious, violent, conceited, often depressed, and full of hate. "I trusted no one. . . . I got lonelier because of my hate. . . . I was sure that love was a lie."

Finally Roberta found a friend who loved her, a friend she could trust.

> I invited Christ into my life personally, and things really began to change. My hatred vanished, and an unexplainable love began to grow for the people I had hated. Because I stopped pitying myself, I was ready to reach out and help people.
>
> I found in Christ a Friend I could totally trust . . . Someone who really cared about me with no selfish motives. I reached the end of my loneliness and unhappiness and reached out to Him. And I discovered that Jesus is still the great Healer . . . not physically, in my case, but emotionally. He healed my wracked-up emotions.

Another thing Roberta found through Christ was more power. In witchcraft she had been obsessed with the idea of getting power; in Christ she found something far better:

> The Holy Spirit provides all of God's good power . . . but it's *power without bondage.* I lived all my life in the occult under an unseen whip that I wouldn't admit to. And I was responsible for many things that were wrong, things that hurt a lot of people. But Jesus offers forgiveness because He died for those things. In

essence, Jesus said after I trusted Him, "Roberta, don't look back."
You know, I never will.

Ron asked Roberta what she thought about young people who
fool around with séances, Ouija boards, and the like, with no in-
tention of getting involved in anything evil. She said that she
knew there were such groups in many high schools, but she also
knew they were playing with something worse than fire:

> Take it from me, those things are much more than fun and
> games. They are the door to a strange world that sucks you right
> in. You taste a little—just for fun—and you want to come back for
> more. You just don't realize how deep you're going or how seri-
> ous it is. That's why the Bible says, "Don't give a place to the
> devil." He needs only a foothold to launch his takeover.

I've been impressed very much in the last few weeks with how
great the gulf is between Christ and Satan—and how sharply we
have to draw the line if we're going to be on the side of God and
Christ. Lois Hoadley Dick of Newton, New Jersey, has told of
her friend Janet who visited a gathering of spiritualists. Terribly
depressed when she arrived and sorry she had come, Janet started
repeating to herself the promise of 1 John 1:7, ". . . the blood of
Jesus Christ his Son, cleanseth us from all sin."

The leader tried several times to begin the séance, without
success. Finally he announced, "There is someone here who is
hindering the service. I cannot do anything until you leave." So
Janet got up and walked out. She realized she had come to a
place where she had no right to be, and apparently the spiritualists could not coexist with the blood of Christ.

Just before the Super Bowl football game in January, 1974, a
group of psychics and astrologers was asked who was going to
win—the Minnesota Vikings or the Miami Dolphins. There was
heavy enthusiasm for a Viking victory, based a lot on Coach Bud
Grant's star signs. "My vibrations tell me that his spirit is going
to prevail," said Houston occultist Sister Rainbow.

Well, those vibrations were wrong. The Vikings fought hard—

but what could they do against that unstoppable Dolphin machine? Some of my Christian friends and I often pray for the players as we watch games like that one. Admiring players on both teams, I wished there were some way *both* sides could win Super Bowl VIII. But of course only one team can win the Vince Lombardi Trophy, and the Dolphins' 24 to 7 victory proved once again that the psychics can be completely wrong.

It's a sign of the times that all that publicity was given to those psychics. Why should it be? Only because so many of us are so gullible that we'll listen to anyone who prattles about planetary conjunctions and mystical vibrations.

The movie *The Exorcist* is a shocking portrayal of the satanic possession of a twelve-year-old girl. Her face, her language and her actions become unspeakably repulsive as the devil takes control of her mind and body. Some of the people who stood in line for hours to see this picture said they wanted to see the child vomit on the priest; others, to see her masturbate with a crucifix. I wonder how many in the crowds who flocked to watch *The Exorcist* knew that it was based on fact. In 1949 a teen-age child in Maryland had a very similar possession, and the demon invader was finally exorcised by a Jesuit priest.

Just as *The Exorcist* was hitting the movie theaters, strange noises frightened workers remodeling a house in Texas. The house, known as "Devil's Corner," was said to have been used for pagan worship. A priest was called in to drive out the demonic presence.

And about the same time, a priest in California told of being called upon for help when a family was harassed by strange incidents. Fires started mysteriously in different parts of the home. Religious statues were destroyed. Knives and glasses sailed through the air when there was nothing to move them. Members of the family felt themselves seized by the throat and knocked unconscious. The priest performed the ceremony of exorcism fourteen times. The Archbishop of San Francisco said that after this the family found peace and relief.

The occult world is a many-headed monster, and every head sprouts from a single source—Satan. Don't fool around with astrology, reincarnation, gurus, spiritualism, inner visions, mystic auras, astral travel, Ouija, witchcraft, or anything of the kind. All of it is from below, not from above—from the devil, not from God.

Today I'm conscious as never before of the way the forces of evil are lined up against the powers of God. I predict that in the months ahead, occultism will enter more and more of our whole society. The stage is being set. In this twentieth century since Jesus came, a lot of people have turned from God to science to solve their problems. Now, with more and more shortages of the things we need, with our scientific achievements threatening to destroy us, men and women realize that science can't solve all their problems either, and they are looking for some other saviour. Strange occult forces beckon. I believe they will continue to trap many more victims. Don't let them trap *you!*

Take no part in the worthless pleasures of evil and darkness, but instead rebuke and expose them.

Ephesians 5:11 LB

7

A Necessary Evil?

While I was speaking at a church college, one student came to see me about a problem. He told me: "You know, in this school you can do just about anything you want to. I've slept with five different girls in the last month. I've got a hang-up on sex. I love it!"

"Sex is a wonderful gift of God," I said. "Why do you want to make it low and dirty?"

"But I don't," this young fellow said. "Sex isn't dirty!"

"Of course it isn't," I said. "Neither is a flower. But if you pull up a beautiful flower by the roots and drop it on your dinner plate, you won't want to eat from that plate until it's washed. There's nothing wrong with the flower—it's just in the wrong place.

"Sex outside of marriage is in the wrong place. I like sex as much as you, but I love Jesus! If you love Him, He has to be first. After you've had sex, how do you feel? During the experience you may feel great because your emotions take over. But afterward, when your mind and your conscience have a chance to get back to work, you know you've done wrong, don't you? You defiled yourself and the girl. Let God keep you clean!"

I know it's not easy to do that in this age, when the devil seems to be using every trick in his book to turn things around and make black look white, and young people especially are exposed to temptations of which our grandparents couldn't have dreamed. Recently a number of people were startled by the frank confessions of a teen-age girl. At thirteen, Joyce Maynard joined a youth group in a liberal church where the young people tried reading the Bible, but—as she reported in an article in the *New York Times Magazine* (April 23, 1972, "An 18-Year-Old Looks Back on Life")—"the Old Testament had no power. We gave up on Genesis and rapped, instead, with a casual college student who started class saying, 'Man, do I have a hangover!'"

Then the group discovered sensitivity training: "Now the group held weekly, nonverbal communication sessions, with lots of hugging and feeling that boosted attendance to triple what it had been in our old save-the-world days."

Marijuana, said Joyce, was smoked by nearly everyone in her high school. "Drugs took on a disproportionate importance. Why was it I could spend half a dozen evenings with someone without his ever asking me what I thought of Beethoven or Picasso but always, in the first half hour, he'd ask me whether I smoked?"

At eighteen Joyce Maynard entered Yale:

> The freshman women's dorm at Yale has no house mother. We have no check-in hours or drinking rules or punishments for having boys in our rooms past midnight. A guard sits by the door to offer, as they assured us at the beginning of the year, physical —not moral—protection. All of which makes it easy for many girls who feel, after high-school curfews and dating regulations, suddenly liberated. (The first week of school last fall, many girls stayed out all night, every night, displaying next morning the circles under their eyes the way some girls show off engagement rings.)
>
> We all received the *Sex at Yale* book, a thick, black pamphlet filled with charts and diagrams and a lengthy discussion of contraceptive methods. And at the first women's assembly, the discussion moved quickly from course-signing-up procedures to gynecology, where it stayed for much of the evening. Somebody raised her hand to ask where she could fill her pill prescription, someone else wanted to know about abortions. There was no standing in the middle any more—you had to either take out a pen and paper

and write down the phone numbers they gave out or stare stonily ahead, implying that those were numbers you certainly wouldn't be needing. From then on in it seemed the line had been drawn.

But of course the problem is that no lines, no barriers, exist. Where, five years ago a girl's decisions were made for her (she had to be in at 12 and, if she was found—in—with her boyfriend . . .); today, the decision rests with her alone. She is surrounded by knowledgeable, sexually experienced girls and if she isn't willing to sleep with her boyfriend, somebody else will. It's peer-group pressure, 1972 style—the embarrassment of virginity.

That's pretty frank language for a Christian book, isn't it? I've quoted it because for too long Christians have been so nicey-nice we haven't dared even talk about some of the real problems of life. And adults haven't had any idea what it's like to grow up in this sex-saturated age.

Let me throw out a few facts:

- A sign on the desk of a college dean asks passing students HAVE YOU HAD YOUR PILL TODAY?

- A college official, asked about students' sexual relationships, answers, "It's no concern of ours who sleeps with whom."

- It is the accepted thing in a number of universities for boys to sleep with their dates in their dormitory rooms on weekends.

- The book *The Student Guide to Sex on Campus* has received official approval on many campuses.

- Some parents let their teen-age children sleep at home with their friends of the opposite sex.

- Less than half of the teen-agers in America are virgins; 70 percent believe there is nothing immoral about sex before marriage.

- An increasing number of young women are having babies outside of marriage, while abortions are at an all-time high.

- Homosexuals and lesbians are making more and more blatant demands for acceptance, recognition, and "equal rights" to employment by groups (such as police and fire departments) which do not tend to welcome such people into their ranks.

- Venereal disease is spreading so fast that it is now recognized as a public epidemic.

- An article appeared in the March 28, 1974 issue of the *Raleigh Times,* a Raleigh, North Carolina newspaper, "Sex Offers Elderly Release From Anxiety." It stated that there should be a more tolerant attitude taken towards the patients in nursing homes. A room should be set aside for sex to offer the elderly the kind of relief that most people get from tranquilizers, alcohol, eating, and violent behavior. We should consider the therapeutic value of sex activity among the elderly. Tolerance should extend to homosexuality and sex between unmarried persons by mutual consent.

When I was speaking in New York recently I took a walk across town. Three young women in extrarevealing dresses smiled their invitations. A burly man and one with slim hips came down the street holding hands. A huckster blared from a doorway, "See the skin flicks. A live sex show after every movie. Everything you ever wanted to know about sex, performed before your eyes!" Bookshop windows were crammed with books and magazines so luridly explicit I felt embarrassed to be near them.

All this may be a bit more blatant in New York than in most cities, but the same kind of thing can be found in every part of the world. There seems to be a never-satisfied demand for more nudity, more sex, more perversion, more debasement. Movies, books, magazines, and shows banned a few years ago seem mild compared to what is produced and shown today.

I've already discussed the pornography so prevalent today. But don't blame the porn merchants alone for all this. Our whole society is sex-crazed, according to more than one observer, and I have to agree. Our moral standards keep slipping.

Venereal disease is on a rampage. Gonorrhea is becoming a national epidemic. Gonorrhea, sometimes called "clap" or "morning dew," can produce heart disease, arthritis, eye inflammation, blood poisoning, and pelvic and intestinal disease. A pregnant girl who has gonorrhea may give birth to a blind child.

The other leading venereal disease—which means disease spread through sexual relations—is syphilis, which is also approaching the epidemic stage. Syphilis may cause paralysis, insanity, blindness, heart disease, sterility, and even death. It too can produce blindness and other diseases in babies.

Venereal disease is passed from one person to another by sexual intercourse (and sometimes by contaminated hypodermic needles). VD is growing and spreading like a monster. It is destroying our teens.

There is a widespread idea today that sex isn't any more important than a handshake, and therefore that most of the laws and principles safeguarding marriage and the home are ready for the scrap heap. In one popular motion picture a group of college students is encouraged in sexual promiscuity by the administration; the words *marriage* and *adultery* are passed off as "no longer meaningful." When one student asks a faculty member why the teacher and her husband don't take part in the school's sexual experiment, she replies that it's up to the new generation to revolutionize sex: "We represent the past. You represent the future."

A British sex-education film aimed at adolescents shows a twenty-three-year-old teacher masturbating and generally endorses promiscuity.

Joyce Maynard is right. The whole idea of sexual purity is so often ridiculed today, and popping into bed with practically anyone is accepted so widely as good and right, that virginity seems embarrassing.

Well, what can we do about it? One of the problems is that Christians sometimes act as though sex is a *necessary evil*—something you have to admit is a fact, but something you say as little about as possible. I know of one young man who came to know the Lord and went to a Bible college. There, late one night, he was sharing his problems and temptations with other students and several ministers. This boy asked for prayer as he confessed the temptations and pressures that came to him sexually. He was stunned when there was a long silence, followed by several criticisms for speaking so frankly. He was stunned most of all because not a single person present would admit that he had any such sexual impulses or needs.

So often sex is presented as though it's unnatural, or at best a means to something else—so seldom as something God created, right and beautiful in the proper setting—a tremendous gift. Christian sex education is so needed today, and so seldom found! When the Bible's teaching about sex is given, too often it is presented through the sins of David and Bathsheba, Solomon, Samson, and so on.

The church ought to emphasize instead the positive side of sex! Think of the normal, happy married life of Abraham and Sarah, Boaz and Ruth, Joseph and Mary. Think of Jesus' presence at the famous wedding in Cana. Think of His words:

> But from the beginning of the creation God made them male and female. For this cause shall a man leave his father and mother, and cleave to his wife; And they twain shall be one flesh: so then they are no more twain, but one flesh. What therefore God hath joined together, let not man put asunder.

> Mark 10:6–9

That is beautiful! Sex at its best, as God meant it to be, is the union and the sharing of two lives in a relationship so intimate and wonderful that it is hard to describe. It is indeed a blessed gift.

But pornographic pictures and movies make sex seem ugly and dirty. They ruin its meaning. All these pictures make a big thing of positions, of the sex act in itself. Such pornography stirs the minds of the mentally ill and degrades the beauty of this gift of God.

I am very disturbed at the attitudes of many people concerning this area. Sinners are not the only ones who know how to make love. Christians are not square! They have human desires and passions like anyone else. I don't have to pray before making love. I can enjoy sex as much as anyone. Sexual relations are very beautiful, thrilling and satisfying—with the right person.

The right person for me is my wife. The right sexual partner for you is your wife or husband. I'm not being preachy when I say that, but there are a lot of hang-ups in evangelists and pastors today. They get so involved in their work that they forget that they have a woman beside them; a woman (their wife) who has a right to be satisfied. They get so tired that they have no time for their wives. They feel so holy that they have no time to touch their wives. This is permissible if husband and wife are fasting, but man and wife should not separate themselves all of the time.

I admit that I can be tempted as much as anyone else. It's like going into a bank. I may wish I had all that money, but that's a long way from holding up the bank or walking out with a stolen roll of hundred-dollar bills in my pocket. I know that money belongs to someone else! I can appreciate the good looks of another woman, but she's not mine and sex outside of marriage is not right, and all the "new morality" in the world will never make it right.

I hear of so many hang-ups from Christian women. Some of them have the wrong concept of marriage. There is nothing in the Bible that tells you that you should do this or that, or that you should not do something else, in the privacy of your marriage. My wife has personal desires. I am her man. She desires to be touched and/or caressed by me. She knows that I am hers and she is mine. She does not have to ask me to make love to her, and she doesn't tell me that she wants me to make love to her: she just provokes me into it. She has no hang-ups in this area because she has a perfect right to be aggressive. Both partners should be aggressive—which makes for a more desirable relationship. There is nothing wrong with a good wife being a "tiger" in bed and a lady on the street. There is also nothing in the Bible that says you should have sexual relations any number of times a month. A couple may have sexual relations as often as they desire. The Bible says to be considerate of the other person's body. Some of the things a wife could do to "turn her husband on" is perhaps to wear a sexy nightgown, have a fresh breath, and have a clean, but not stifling, fragrance. Bad odors are repulsive.

Jesus does not teach us techniques. When two people are joined together in the sight of God in holy matrimony, they become one. No position nor method of intercourse is wrong. It is not my business to tell anyone how to make love—I'm only saying that anything a husband and wife do during their intimate times together is acceptable to God. You don't have to read a dirty book or see a dirty film to get turned on. Some adults actually do this and then switch husbands and wives to satisfy their physical desires. This is all wrong!

Many books are written, filled with a lot of advice on how to make love. I will not accept any such book nor watch any film of this kind.

The intimate relationship between husband and wife in sex is beautiful. There is nothing in any way filthy or ugly about it. The human body is to be desired and enjoyed in the marital act. Sex is like a fine dessert after a good meal—without any calories.

Thank God for this marvelous gift of sex. Don't let anything cheapen it for you or yours. Real committed Christian marriages witness to the fact that sex enjoyment went way up after Christ was the center of their marriage. Many Spirit-filled Christian couples are testifying to this great truth and witnessing to new pleasure in sex life as their marriage in Christ grows.

Young Christian wives and husbands also witness to the teachings of Jesus in the Bible that will make them more attractive to each other. A man or woman who loves the Lord can be taught by God Himself to be more beautiful to his or her spouse than ever before.

8

Gay Isn't Happy

It was the end of a crusade I had held in a famous tourist city. Most of the young people who had come forward to talk to me had gone home. Then a teen-age girl I had noticed waiting at one side came up to me.

She was one of the most beautiful girls I have ever seen. While she began speaking, a reporter from the local daily kept looking at her as though he'd been bewitched. A cleaning man crossed the coliseum with his broom—and turned back, unable to tear his eyes away from this girl's face. Three young men who had started out the door came back and stared.

"Nicky," she said, tossing her long golden hair out of her blue eyes, "I dig guys. Girls too. What's wrong with that?"

"You mean sex?" I said. I knew what her answer would be.

"Sure," she said. "I'm bisexual. I like it. What's wrong with it?"

"Why do you ask me?"

"Well . . .", she stopped. "I liked what you said tonight. I guess the way I live doesn't fit, you know, what you said about accepting Jesus."

"You've got it!" I went over the Gospel again in a few words. "You'll have to choose between Jesus and whatever takes the place of Jesus in your life."

"It's not easy," she said with tears in the blue eyes. "I'd like to give my life to Jesus, but sex is so strong."

"Very strong. But if you take Jesus, you're not on your own. Keep close to Him, and He'll help you every step of the way."

I prayed with this girl. Before she stopped praying, she was crying, and there were tears in my eyes, too. I could feel God struggling with Satan for the soul of that girl, and it was a beautiful moment when she cried out, "Praise the Lord!" I knew she was delivered. A letter from her just a few days ago contained this sentence:

> Ever since that night I found Christ, there has been a real difference in my life. I've been tempted to go back to the old ways, many times, but every time Jesus has given me the victory. They say lesbians and gays can't be changed. Well, Jesus has made me a completely new person.

Homosexuality isn't new, but it used to be underground. Today it is coming out into the open. All over the world, gays are campaigning for recognition and acceptance. They have their own clubs and bars. They are turning out propaganda to make their twisted attitude toward life look normal and right. At a recent meeting of the National Education Association, one teacher announced a gay caucus.

And—God help us!—the homosexuals are even creating their own gay *churches*. When such a church was chartered recently in Boston, one minister stood with his arm around his homosexual lover, while another minister, a woman, embraced her lesbian mate. At the Communion service that followed, the gay lovers present were invited to take the Communion elements together.

The worshipers in a New York church were startled one Sunday morning to see behind the altar a large painting of two nude homosexual couples. The painting was there as a backdrop for a play about homosexuality that was performed soon afterward at the church.

Early in 1974 a national magazine printed a news item about a school for homosexuals that opened in San Francisco. This school has been flooded with requests for information on how to enroll. In the same magazine there was a news report about the gay "marriage" of two black men. Only a year before, the male "bride" had entered into another homosexual union that (like many such alliances) lasted only a short time.

Things like this are becoming so common nowadays that they are hardly news any more—unless they're connected with something supersensational. Recently the worst mass murders in history were uncovered near Houston, Texas. A detective said, "The place was wall-to-wall bodies." Investigators dug up the corpses of dozens of young men who had been homosexually assaulted and tortured. Soon after that, a nationwide homosexual ring was discovered operating out of another city. The operators published pictures and descriptions of young boys for the benefit of men all over the country who were the "customers." Some of the pictures found at the gang's headquarters had the word KILL written across them. The reason: these particular boys had been "unco-operative."

There's a tide of permissiveness today, a trend to accept any kind of sexual deviation and label it normal and right. I was asked to speak to my own state legislature recently when a bill was introduced to legalize practically all forms of sexual behavior except rape. Let me make it clear where I stand on such things. There is no question that in God's eyes homosexuality is not right, it is not just a sickness, *it is dead wrong.* That's what the Bible says in many references, and if you're a Christian you have to accept what the Bible says. Homosexuality is a sin—I'll say more about this later—and the wages of sin is death. Often, death very literally, as the news reports I've referred to show.

But homosexuality, like anything else, doesn't just happen. Why is it increasing today? One reason is what is happening in the home. Families are not what they used to be. Too many fathers, and mothers too, are gone from home too often. When a boy has no strong father to look up to and model his life after, when a girl doesn't learn from her mother how a woman should live, when children have to be on their own, emotionally, too early, they can become confused and grow up with distorted attitudes and confused values.

I am led to say this to all parents: Don't destroy your children by neglect, or by overprotection either. Smother love can cripple your son or daughter. Mother, your first duty is to be a good wife to your husband and mother to your children. Father, you need to be a strong husband and father as the New Testament says, and your children ought to know that you love your wife. A good Christian home is the key to a good future for your children. Today's crop of gays and freaks is the harvest from homes where God was forgotten.

There are so many bad vibrations today! I feel sick when I hear about children being brought up by "parents" of the same sex. And I believe in justice for women, but I don't believe we should pretend women are just like men. There's a difference, in spite of what some of the Women's Libbers say. When girls and boys are dressed and treated exactly alike, when parents push girls into boys' sports and give boys dolls to play with, children are going to be confused about whether they are masculine or feminine. That's the way gays can be programmed.

I'm convinced that homosexuality is often the result of demon possession. When anyone worships sex or other pleasures, the demon of lust has the perfect opportunity to take control. I was impressed by that fact when I met Astra (as I'll call her). This girl was brought up in a home scarred by divorce and drink. In high school she got into drugs and lesbianism. Realizing she needed help, Astra tried sensitivity training, Synanon, and psychotherapy. One of her counselors told this girl her twisted lifestyle was okay and advised her to adjust to it.

But Astra felt possessed by a frightening superhuman power. Fortunately, there were Christians in her school and they let Astra know that they loved her in spite of her habits. They really wanted to help her, so they invited her to a rally I held in the area. At invitation time Astra came forward and accepted Christ.

Astra found an amazing new reality: the love and power of God. Praying, reading the Bible, and attending church and enjoying Christian fellowship were now like food and drink to her.

Her old turmoil and confusion dropped away. Astra says: "I can't believe how God has changed me. What really happened is, Jesus healed me, and now I'm straight and whole!"

Barbara Evans (not her real name, either) has another thrilling story. While she was living with a lesbian friend, Barbara read Pat Boone's book *A New Song* and felt compelled to write to him. Pat wrote back, and a remarkable correspondence developed between the confused girl and Pat, the earnest Christian. Barbara Evans's story in *Joy!* shows how Pat's concern led this girl out of her homosexual trap.

Barbara Evans finally reached the point where she was able to love her former lesbian roommate, not with the old lust, but with the pure love of God. In one of her last letters in *Joy!* she wrote to Pat Boone:

> Pat, do you remember that in your first letter you said God would purify my love for my friend? . . . *For the first time in ten years I was able to hug the one whom I had loved in the flesh in the purity of God's love. Praise the Almighty and Everlasting God!*
>
> No one can realize what a tremendous change has come about in my life. Since I was sixteen, I was obsessed with the desire to love and be loved by my friend. I went through years of torture —waiting, hoping, believing and even praying that someday the love I felt deep within would be returned. In all that time I never knew that the person I was really searching for was Jesus Christ, the Son of the Living God. Only when God opened my eyes which had been blinded by Satan did I discover that there was something desperately wrong in my life. When I finally admitted it and gave up my life, I found what my whole being had craved and ached for—Jesus! Praise God that "ye shall know the truth, and the truth shall make you free."
>
> Oh, Pat, *it is so important that people who have a homosexual hang-up realize that Jesus is their only answer.* (Reprinted with permission from *Joy! A Homosexual's Search for Fulfillment* by Pat Boone. © 1973 by Creation House, 499 Gunderson, Carol Stream, Illinois 60187.)

Right on! God hates homosexuality, but He loves homosexuals as much as anyone else. If you are not convinced whether homosexuality is right or wrong, let me tell you about two men who spent the night in a city with a wild reputation. The two visitors were straight. A lot of the men in the city were openly gay. When they heard that there were visitors in town, they shouted, "Bring out those men to us so we can rape them."

The man who owned the house where the visitors were staying told the gays, "Please, fellows, don't do such a wicked thing. Look —I have two virgin daughters, and I'll surrender them to you to do with as you wish. But leave these men alone!"

The gays wouldn't listen. So full of unnatural lust they weren't satisfied with the substitute, they tried to break into the house to attack the visitors.

What happened next you will find in Genesis 19: 10–25. (The above conversation is from the *Living Bible* paraphrase, verses 4–9.) Fire fell from heaven on that wicked city and it went up in smoke and destruction. If you wanted to see the city's remains today you would have to fly to Israel and look underneath the Dead Sea. The city's name was Sodom—a name forever after linked with depraved sex. The fate of the immoral cities of Sodom and Gomorrah is a warning of the fate that lies ahead for Sodomites, Lesbians, and others who cling to homosexual sin instead of to Christ.

If you want to know more about the real meaning of homosexuality, read the first chapter of Romans. There you'll see the descent of man into pride, idolatry and gross sin.

Because men are such fools, God has given them over to do the filthy things their hearts desire, and they do shameful things with each other. . . . God has given them over to shameful passions. Even the women pervert the natural use of their sex into unnatural acts. In the same way the men give up natural sexual relations with women and burn with passion for each other. [They] do shameful things with each other, and as a result they receive in themselves the punishment they deserve for their wrongdoing.

Romans 1:24, 26, 27 TEV

No, for anyone who takes God and His Word seriously, there is no question that homosexuality is a vile sin, utterly wrong.

Yet God loves every sinner. If you have been caught in the homosexual trap, you may already realize that it is a deadly trap and that few escape. I know of only one way out—through Jesus Christ! He is big enough and loving enough and strong enough to get you out and make you over. Turn to Him this minute, before it's too late. You'll be amazed at what He can do.

One thing about homosexuals that hits me is this: *gay isn't happy.* Of all the sad, hopeless, miserable people I've ever seen, the gays are among the saddest and most miserable. They may tell themselves they are really free and enjoying life, but deep down they know it's a lie. The real joy comes when they find Jesus.

A final word to Christians. Don't think that being a Christian lifts you above the homosexual temptations. I knew a preacher in a large northwestern city who testified how God had delivered him from homosexuality and other sins. Yet one day as I was sitting in his study talking with this man, he made advances which indicated that the demon of homosexuality was back in his life. I rebuked that evil spirit. This man confessed that slowly he had gotten further and further away from Christ, until finally his old habit had crept back into his life.

A few weeks later that preacher had a real experience with Christ. He confessed to Him his weakness and sin, and Jesus gave him complete, total victory over his old habit. Today he's one of the happiest men I've ever seen. He's found where real joy and satisfaction are—in God and Jesus and the Holy Spirit.

9

Religion

You may be surprised to find a chapter on religion in a book about corruption. Most people seem to think anything religious is good. That isn't necessarily so.

Only one step away from the occult are the pseudoreligions that seem to be blossoming all over the world today. Many of them are doing very well. The Process Church of the Final Judgement, one of the newest religions on the American scene, incredibly combines worship of Jesus with worship of Satan. Its members aggressively hunt for converts on city streets and college campuses, and it has already received so much support that it has leased a valuable building in the middle of New York City as headquarters. Obviously, all this wouldn't be happening if the Process leaders weren't very persuasive and if a good many people weren't ready for a completely new religion, even if it does make a god of the devil.

Every year the Eastern religions fare better in the Western Hemisphere. A whole procession of gurus from India have hit it big in the United States. One of the most successful right now is teen-aged Maharaj Ji, who had six American followers in 1971 and now has so many that his movement, the Divine Light Mission, has an annual budget of three million dollars and has "missions" in thirty-seven countries. (There are more than six million followers of Maharaj Ji in India alone.) To these followers, Maharaj Ji is "The Perfect Living Master." Rennie Davis, just a little while ago a radical revolutionary, is now a convert. He says Maharaj Ji appeared to him in a vision with the words, "I am your Lord," and Rennie is one of the many who have left all else to follow him.

Late in 1973, members of the Divine Light Mission rented the Houston Astrodome to praise Maharaj Ji and celebrate "Millennium '73" which was supposed to bring peace to the world through its teen-aged lord. The Mission plans to build its own divine city in this country, run on solar energy and designed to fulfill practically all its inhabitants' desires at the touch of a button.

Another popular new religion is Scientology, founded by an American science-fiction writer named L. Ron Hubbard. The basic philosophy here is dianetics, a sort of science-fiction version of self-psychoanalysis. Through certain routines—sold to initiates at fifteen dollars-and-up an hour—a person becomes *cleared* of his problems and hang-ups and is supposed to end up feeling good toward everybody and confident that he can do practically anything. From the appearance of some of the seedy-looking people I've seen handing out Scientology literature, I find it hard to believe they are *clears*. And as far as goodwill toward other people is concerned, both Scientologists and Maharajjiologists can be very vindictive toward anyone who criticizes—or even tells the truth about—their religion. One newspaperman was beaten up so severely after publishing an unfavorable story about Maharaj Ji that he had to have a steel plate put in his fractured skull.

When *Newsweek* said recently that the world seems to be looking for new gods to worship, it was commenting on one of the great movements of our time. Everywhere people are searching for something, someone to believe in, and they fill the empty place in the center of their hearts with whatever substitutes they can find for the God who is revealed in Jesus Christ. And I'm concerned about the many religions, new and old, that are luring so many people today. Christian churches are being crowded out by temples of Buddhism and Islam and other cults. A new Japanese religion, Soka Gakkai, has grown from five thousand members to ten million in less than thirty years. Another Japanese group making headway in America is the Church of Perfect Liberty, which lets its members have their cake and eat it too. This church teaches that playing golf is a way of self-improvement. Members don't need to skip church to play golf on Sunday mornings; they can do both at the same time!

On almost any city street or college campus today you can see Hare Krishna converts dancing and chanting, handing out literature and even food consecrated before their idols. I must say they show a lot of zeal and courage, to spend so much time dancing barefoot in their saffron robes, to shave their heads and paint their foreheads, and do more public witnessing every day than many Christian church members do in a lifetime. And it seems to be paying off. This religious order has grown so fast in one American city that it is shopping around for a building for its headquarters, and payment seems to be no problem.

A minister friend told me of running into a Hare Krishna group celebrating just off Times Square, which is sometimes called "the crossroads of the world." At an intersection, incense burned in front of what looked something like a large dollhouse with figures that looked like a doll and a toy elephant inside.

"What is that?" my friend asked one of the whirling Hare Krishna youngsters.

"That," she replied, "is God."

"*God?*" he asked.

"Yes. If you accept it, that is God. The two figures are the male and female personifications of the infinite force of the universe." Then, watching my friend's face and probably realizing he wasn't going to be a believer, she added: "But if you do not accept it, those are just two dolls."

"I got an eerie feeling," my friend said as he told me about the incident, "realizing that those Eastern idols were being worshiped in the middle of America's largest city!"

In Iceland there is a revival of the old worship of Thor, Odin, Loki, and other gods and goddesses of ancient Norse mythology. Before Christianity came to Scandinavia, human sacrifices were made to these gods. The new worshipers are trying to get permission to make sacrifices of horses and to brew their own spirits for their services, and have announced that their aim is to de-Christianize all Iceland.

It could spread. If you see a bunch of people in animal skins burning a horse on a funeral pyre and drinking aquavit, it may be just one more new-old religious gathering—this time out of Scandinavian mythology.

"So what?" you may ask. "These religions don't harm anybody, do they?" Don't be too sure about that. For example, Scientologists are taught: "Never fear to hurt another in a just cause." Doesn't that remind you a little of Adolf Hitler—or the Communists—or Watergate?

In the summer of 1973 a faith healer laid his hands on the head of an eleven-year-old boy with diabetes and someone shouted, "Praise the Lord! He's healed!" The next day when the boy went into the kitchen to take his regular insulin shot, his father broke the needle and threw it away. For a short time the boy was happy —no more shots, and he could eat all the cake and ice cream he wanted. But in two days he was dead.

I know God can do miracles, but it's dangerous to turn our backs on the tools of healing which He puts in our hands. God and medicine aren't enemies; they're allies in the fight against disease and death, as thousands of Christian doctors and their patients know. The wonderful thing about Christ's healing is that it begins where medicine ends. But it is a corruption of faith to reject God's gifts of medical and scientific knowledge.

So religion can be a corruptor and destroyer, too! The religious establishment ganged up with nonreligious groups to crucify Christ. Religion has bad things as well as good things connected with it. Wars have been started, "heretics" have been tortured, martyrs have endured agonizing deaths—all in the name of religion.

I'm not saying Christianity is perfect, either. The Christian churches have had their share of corruption down through the ages. At one time, when one church controlled most of Europe, there were so many orgies, prostitutes, bribes, illegitimate chil-

dren, and murders even at the highest levels of church government that the period is often called the Rule of the Harlots. You
can't say Roman Catholics had a corner on such things, either.
Protestants have had their share of wars and tortures and heresy
trials and brainwashing and corruption. And before the division
between Protestants and Catholics, losing a religious debate
could mean being thrown out of the country or being killed.

The thing that is important is not religion but *Jesus. He* is not
a religion. *He* is a living experience. The one thing that can make
our churches vital and real to people is to help them turn away
from empty, dead religious traditions and controversies, to the
living experience of Jesus Christ—as so many are doing.

There is one religious movement today that is amazing everyone who sees it—the Jesus Movement among young people all
over the world. Many of these youngsters have turned away from
the programs of the established churches, but have *turned on to
Jesus*. Some have founded their own churches, electing their own
deacons and elders and conducting their own services. Perhaps
some of these groups have gone to dangerous extremes, but wherever I see people who love Jesus, I feel I'm among friends. To
me the Jesus Movement is a marvelous example of how God's
Spirit is working today, though often clear outside the organized
churches.

In Ann Arbor, Michigan, the Word of God Community holds
praise and prayer meetings every Thursday night; hundreds of
young people attend regularly. One of the hymns they often sing
goes like this:

> The Holy Ghost will set your feet a-dancing
> The Holy Ghost will thrill you through and through
> The Holy Ghost will set your feet a-dancing
> And set your heart a-dancing too.

It seems to me that's typical of the new Jesus Movement.
There's not a thing dull or stuffy or stodgy about it. It sets hearts
dancing! And it shows the *power* of the Spirit of God. Time and

again, drug addicts who find Jesus through groups of this kind, gain deliverance from drugs so quickly that observers find it incredible.

Sometimes—though not always—addicts who come to Jesus kick their habits with no withdrawal symptoms whatsoever. When other young people see that happening, they don't need someone to convince them that Jesus is real and alive today. They *know* it! They have seen Him at work! I have, too.

And that's the whole key to "destructive" religion. When Jesus isn't a vital part of it, there can be a very corruptive influence.

It's amazing what most religions really think about Jesus and God and even about life. According to many of them, life is a pretty rotten deal controlled by inexplicable fate, with no real hope, no real security. God is only a name for some kind of abstract force or power. And Jesus is just one more teacher or guru or saviour. *All the non-Christian religions deny that He is the unique Saviour and God that He tells us He is.* All of them deny that Jesus is the only way to God, that His blood atones for our sins, and that He is the only genuine bridge between sinful humans and a holy God. They can't admit that Jesus is Lord of lords and King of kings.

Nearly every one of the new religions tries to drag Jesus down to a purely human level, to put Him on the same level as Buddha and Confucius and Mohammed and a whole group of other beings.

None of those religions helped me when I was hooked on hatred and crime. Most of them have great-sounding rituals and rules and good advice. But they don't show you how to find help when you're up against it. Jesus did and does, and that's why I'll stand with Him against anyone who denies what He says:

> I am the Way—yes, and the Truth and the Life. No one can get to the Father except by means of me.

John 14:6 LB

Go in by the narrow gate. For the wide gate has a broad road which leads to disaster, and there are many people going that way. The narrow gate and the hard road lead out into life, and only a few are finding it.

Matthew 7:13, 14 PHILLIPS

Come to me, all of you who are tired from carrying your heavy loads, and I will give you rest. Take my yoke and put it on you, and learn from me, for I am gentle and humble in spirit; and you will find rest. The yoke I will give you is easy, and the load I will put on you is light.

Matthew 11:28–30 TEV

10

Money, Money, Money

After Bobby Fischer won the world chess championship, Russian newspapers denounced his delay in agreeing to a rematch with the Soviet champion. They said Bobby Fischer's only motivation was "money, money and money." They questioned his love of chess and called him a "chess-businessman"—probably the worst word anyone in a Communist country could use. As a matter of fact, Fischer seems to have been holding out for a million-dollar prize for the winner, and that looks like an awful lot of money until you start thinking of how much money so many other people with a lot less talent than Bobby Fischer are making.

When athletes and entertainers are paid many times more than presidents, when public officials become millionaires while in offices where it is said that the expenses are greater than the salary, when the highest-paid police in America are reported to make more than their salaries from bribes, when the primary (and practically only) consideration in business is profit, something is wrong. Money isn't the root of all evil, as some people think the Bible says. But "the *love* of money is a source of all kinds of evil" (*see* 1 Timothy 6:10 TEV—*italics* added). When anyone loves money instead of people and God, he's in deep spiritual trouble. Nobody can really afford to be motivated only by money, money, money.

And yet every one of us knows how important money is in

these days of shortages and inflation. We can't do without money but we have to learn to live with it and escape being corrupted by it.

Not long ago a woman telephoned me to ask for an appointment for her boss to see me. If you heard his name you would recognize him as head of one of the most successful businesses in his area. After he arrived, his uniformed chauffeur waited in the parking lot in an enormous Lincoln Continental during the visit.

"What's wrong with me?" the executive asked. "Every night this month I've lain awake for hours dreading the morning. A week ago I was in Chicago on a business trip and I had the strongest urge to throw myself out my hotel window. There's nothing I can think of that I couldn't buy if I wanted it—and there's nothing I want to buy."

It was incredible! Here was one of the richest businessmen I know, asking me, Nicky Cruz, a onetime slum kid, for help. What could I say? What would you have said to this man? Think that over while I mention a couple of other things about this subject of money.

You may be waiting for me to knock money. I'm not going to. I know how important it is—and so do you. You know you can't get along without that indispensable "green stuff." You can't do much of anything or go hardly anywhere, you can't live, and you can't even die decently without money. And let's face it, even in church you have to think about what to put in the collection plate.

In a way, money is life. It takes sweat and muscle power and brainpower to get money, and all kinds of good things in life are bought with money. There was a businessman named Russell Conwell who raised many thousands of dollars to found Temple University in Philadelphia, and in a famous speech, "Acres of Diamonds," he said:

> Money is power, and you ought to be reasonably ambitious to have it. You ought because you can do more good with it than you could without it. Money printed your Bible, money builds

your churches, money sends your missionaries, and money pays
your preachers, and you would not have many of them, either,
if you did not pay them. . . . The man who gets the largest
salary can do the most good with the power that is furnished to
him.

Of course, money doesn't necessarily do all that good. Here in
America today we spend $40 billion a year to travel, $9 billion to
eat out, $6 billion to drink, more than $3 billion in beauty shops.
We spend more for liquor than for milk or education, more for
tobacco than for bread, more for gambling than for meat, more
than twice as much for jewelry and movies as everything we give
to the churches.

These days you can even buy cosmetics for dogs. One chain of
department stores offers poodle perfume, nail polish, and mascara—"for sophisticated dogs, slate gray to accent their liquid
eyes."

Think of that the next time you break a ten-dollar bill!

But what I really want to say about money is to warn you to
watch out for the power it can gain over you. It is important to
have a job in which you can make a living and serve God. But
too often making a living becomes the big thing in our minds.
And then, to keep the paycheck coming, we can find ourselves in
a corner where we think we must do something which we know
deep down is wrong.

Have you heard about Frank Serpico? As a boy in New York
he dreamed of helping people by becoming a policeman. Then
when he got on the police force he discovered that too many of
his buddies were taking bribes on the side. Some of them said
they took only "clean" bribes. "Clean" meant payoffs for traffic
violations or gambling or prostitution. "Dirty money" meant
bribes from the drug business. (Some of the police, Serpico noticed, took payoffs from the drug pushers, too, when the bribes
were big and juicy enough.)

Serpico didn't like any of this. He decided to live only on his
policeman's salary, which was an embarrassment to others who
received substantial portions of their income from the criminal

world which they were supposed to police. When a special commission started looking into corruption among the police and Serpico was questioned, he told the truth. That, of course, was even more embarrassing to everyone involved in taking bribes or just looking the other way when the payola was distributed. Serpico heard that the word had gone out to get him. He got used to hearing threats like "if he isn't careful he'll be found face down in the East River."

Serpico went on about his business. Six months after he told the truth in a trial, he started out with two other policemen to capture a heroin pusher, in the Williamsburg section of Brooklyn. Dressed in high boots, dungarees, a turtleneck sweater and an old army jacket topped with a scarf, Serpico sauntered into the five-story building where the pusher worked. Underneath the army jacket Serpico had a Browning automatic and a .38. Inside a gas mask which he carried over one shoulder he had his service revolver.

Pretending to be in need of a fix, Serpico knocked on the pusher's door and said in Spanish, "I need something." Behind him his two police companions stood on the landing of the stairs. The door started to open and stopped, checked by a chain lock. Serpico charged into the door, snapped the chain—and found himself pinned, as someone inside jammed the door against him while the pusher raced into another room for his gun.

The pusher shot Serpico in the head while the other cops still stood on the stairs. After he crashed to the floor they appeared and eventually got him to a hospital.

Miraculously, Serpico survived. But during the long weeks in the hospital, the police on guard hardly ever spoke to him. He knew that a number of his fellow officers despised him. A nurse heard one guard say to his relief, "Don't talk to him. He's no good."

Frank Serpico got two sympathy cards while he lay in that New York hospital. One message was a get-well note with the printed hope that the recipient would RECUPERATE QUICKLY! The word "Recuperate" was crossed out and the sender had written in *Die!* The second card read: WITH SINCERE SYMPATHY but underneath was scrawled the regret: *That you didn't get your brains blown out, you rat. . . . Happy Relapse.* Finally, Frank Serpico left the police force. It wasn't too healthy for him around his old beat.

As I write this, a movie about Serpico has just been released. Nothing I've said here is an endorsement of the movie or a blanket approval of everything Serpico may have done. But it is my tribute to a man who had the guts to be a *man,* the strength to be honest when so many others had their hands out for bribes from crooks.

As far as I know, money never corrupted Serpico, but it can corrupt anyone, young or old. When one teen-ager took a job in a supermarket, his boss told him, "Charge the customers a few cents extra whenever you can get away with it. If they catch you at it, apologize and tell them you made a mistake." The boy did it because he didn't want to lose the job.

A secretary may say that her employer is in conference when he isn't because that is part of her job. A government official may falsify records because he understands that to be part of his duties. An engineer may do nothing about the defective steering in a certain automobile because he believes that his company wants him to cover it up. In every case, what is really happening is that something wrong is being done for the sake of money.

To get back to that businessman who came to see me: I found out that although he had a lovely home, a private plane, and considerable investments—all the things so many men and women pour out their lives for—he owned nothing really important. He hadn't been inside a church for years. His children were strangers to him. His wife had been showered with *things* but robbed of the personal attention and love she deserved. So she, like the children, had grown cold and hard toward this man. The result: depression and thoughts of suicide.

I talked with this man for some time. I said, "You have sacrificed your wife's happiness and your children's happiness. And you have lost the best things there are—love and faith and hope. But you still have one thing that you can't buy and you can't lose. Whatever you do, remember this: Jesus loves you!"

We prayed together, and when this businessman left, there

were tears in his eyes. I could see the love of God beginning to get through to him. He was beginning to discover the riches beyond money or price.

As I write this book, the ugly stains of Watergate keep spreading like a foul flood. What was Watergate all about? Money, money, money! So many dollars stuck to so many sticky fingers that laws, morality, and human decency were stepped on and left in the mud. Of course, a lot of things connected with Watergate were not new, but I doubt that ever before in history was so much money used to corrupt so many lives and institutions. Public Enemy Number One may well turn out to be the dollar bill. When one of the officials questioned by the Senate's Watergate Committee was asked why he thought so much corruption had come about, he replied in effect: "Too much money. There were so many millions of dollars with so little restraint on how they could be spent."

Today it seems like money can buy practically anything and anyone. One man protested about what he knew was going on in a certain charitable organization—what was going on bothered his conscience—but he admitted later, "Every time I said something, they shut me up with a raise."

Another man refused to be silenced. When he was ordered to falsify the tax records for a music company, he refused—and was fired. He learned that being true to your principles may cancel your paycheck.

For the worst example of all, look at the way organized crime corrupts everything it touches. Here is the love of money exposed in its nakedest, most horrible form—stopping at nothing from robbery and bribery to torture and murder—as its tentacles grab businessmen and their concerns, public servants and their governments, labor unions, every possible kind of person and organization.

Even the church—even religion! Yes, the love of money can corrupt the highest and best things of all. In the next chapter, I'll give you some examples.

11

The Jesus Money Tree

It's going to be hard to write this chapter, because it will seem to some people that I am knocking other Christian workers. I'm not. But God won't let me write this book without saying what He has told me, so here goes.

Let me start with Rick. The first time I saw him I was just getting started in my ministry. Fresh out of Bible college, I searched for a headquarters. God showed me the place: the middle of a ghetto in Los Angeles with about ten blacks and two or three Mexicans and Asiatics to every white person. There was an old white house on Twentieth Street that looked just right. Some people might call it a white elephant. I loved it because it had plenty of rooms! Rooms for wanderers and drug addicts to find a home and kick their bad habits; rooms where society's outcasts could live and pray and reach out for others; room for God to work.

Out of all the savings I had ever been able to put in the bank, I made the down payment for that first Outreach Center on Twentieth Street.

When we started, the air on Twentieth Street was filled with despair. I was a young Puerto Rican who could barely speak English and no idea of all I was getting into, but I had a vision and a hope. I knew what Jesus had done for me, and I knew what He could do for anyone I could introduce to Him.

Sometimes hope was about all I could offer the houseful of dropouts and addicts I gathered together in that crumbling old house. I remember once for a whole week all we had to eat were stale doughnuts donated by a local bakery. (To this day doughnuts don't get a bit of rise from me; if I were wrecked for a week on a desert island with no food but doughnuts, I don't think I'd eat a thing all week.) Those were the days when drug addiction was largely a ghetto problem; it hadn't yet reached into white suburban society to any great extent, and so many people didn't understand my vision (or chose not to). But on Sundays the members of our little household of hope would go out and speak in small churches, and Christians touched by the Spirit would give us small love offerings for our ministry, and bring us canned food.

But limited as the diet was in the old house on Twentieth Street, we lived life to the fullest degree. It was a house of lonely, hardened children of the streets struggling to get their lives together, knowing that this was the last stop on the way out. And little by little it happened. The Spirit of God reached into those wrecked lives and made them new again. I had been where those young people had been, and in my eyes every boy was me.

Rick had been in trouble with the law so much and busted so many times I think even he had lost count. He was living on Sunset Strip, on drugs, when he found our center. In all his eighteen years he hadn't been able to find an answer to his questions about existence. But he was tired of rebelling against the world and himself and God, and when he found our little community with a living Christ right in the middle of it all, he recognized immediately that Jesus was the answer to all his questions.

In a prayer room that had once been a bank vault, Rick turned his life over to Jesus Christ. He gave Jesus everything—his failures, his drug habits, his attitude (a penal-institution outlook, hardened by too many stretches in reformatories and prisons), his mind, body, and soul. And Jesus really saved him. Some people talk about being saved from sin. Rick *knows* he was completely transformed. "It was so great," Rick says now, "I could feel it in

my bones, and I still can. Jesus reached me when no one else
could."

Rick was one of those people, like St. Paul, who couldn't do
enough for the Christ he had once kicked against. So when he
met established Christians who "looked Christian" but didn't feel
the pull he did to work every minute for the Saviour, he couldn't
understand it. Rick entered Bible college so he could be prepared
for full-time Christian work, and there too he was bothered by
the apathy he found. The other students might study all day and
then turn on the radio and take it easy in the evening. Not Rick!
He wanted to be out witnessing every minute. "Man," he kept
thinking, "there are people dying out there and they need Jesus.
When are we going to put 'Go ye therefore' into high gear?" I
remember that Rick told me he saw so many people looking at
little hills when there were mountains to climb.

Then it happened. All of a sudden Christianity was kicked into
high gear—no, not kicked, slammed. All over the world, thousands
of people began finding Jesus. Junkies, cons, freaks, prostitutes,
businessmen, secretaries, movie stars, housewives, high school
and college students were being saved. At first Rick couldn't believe it. When he picked up a magazine with a photograph of
hundreds of people being baptized in the ocean, Rick cried, "The
revival! It's come!"

The next year books, magazines, television, movies, and newspapers were talking about Jesus. "Christian" became not how you
look but *where you are at.* Jesus festivals were held, books and
magazines began featuring Jesus and the Christian life, Christian
music stood up and started dancing in the aisles!

But as the Christian revival has continued, some things worry
Rick and me. At an evangelistic meeting one of the leaders was
defensive about the fact that nearly everyone present was already
a Christian. He said to me, "Brother, the Lord knew who needed
to be here tonight." I don't accept that. I know that no effort was
made to get unsaved people to come. I'm concerned at the indif-
ference, the lack of direction in our spiritual enthusiasm.

On the other hand, there is the attitude that because you have come to a meeting, something is supposed to happen. I call it *spiritual bloodsucking*. People are invited to a meeting and then drained of everything the leaders can get out of them. It's like using Jesus to get money from people.

Often no one asks, "Why are we doing this?" Instead someone says: "Do it! It will work!" Some religious leaders seem to be selling Jesus the way a sharp salesman sells cars or real estate. Secondary things are put first and primary things seem to be forgotten.

In the evangelistic field today, to be successful, it seems that you have to have a different gimmick or ministry. Instead of preaching Jesus, some evangelists are always selling things. I know of one man who took the tent he had preached under and had it cut into pieces which he sold for a hundred dollars apiece. "The glory of God went through this tent," he claimed, "and you can buy a piece of it." Another evangelist claimed he could sell "angels of light." All kinds of psychological and advertising tricks are used to cheat credulous people.

Two salesmen for a commercial organization came to my office and tried to sell me on the idea of marketing a T-shirt with my name and these words printed on it: SMILE, JESUS LOVES YOU! They told me of the thousands of dollars I would make from this venture, but I sensed a satanic temptation. I thought of the time when Jesus went into the temple and cast out everyone who was buying and selling, and overthrew the money tables. I was led to rebuke these men for their scheme. I did not give my life to Christ for the purpose of making money. In our Outreach ministry, all receipts from crusades go directly to the organization to help with our work. Proceeds from the sale of books and records go directly for the ministry. We do not take any of this money for ourselves. (Royalties from my books, on the other hand, are set aside for my children's education. I do not want my children ever to feel that the Lord forgot to take care of them.) All offerings are turned over to the work of Nicky Cruz Outreach.

We need to be careful that in our honest enthusiasm we don't buy and sell and organize Jesus until we expect Him to react to what *we* want instead of what *He* wants.

And we need to be *very* careful not to make Jesus into a magic money tree. So often, successful entertainers and businessmen are asked to give Christian testimony whereas a plain ordinary Christian who is not making all that money is completely overlooked—even though he might have a lot more to contribute, and much more valuable spiritual insight. It's not meant that way, I'm sure, but the impression is given that accepting Christ is a quick way to fame and fortune.

It isn't.

And how much harm some of these successful "Christian" performers do. There is one well-known religious music group, invited to a good many churches and evangelistic campaigns, which uses gospel music purely to make money. At one of their performances I noticed the eyes of some of these performers roving over the audience as they sang. Then, after the meeting was over, several of the singers took off on dates with the most attractive chicks. Some religious singers perform very well, and dress beautifully, but how they live is what counts. They know the words of the Christian songs, but if someone asked them how to find Jesus Christ, could they do it? I doubt it.

Religion is big business today! Sometimes I wonder about all those Christian buttons and bumper stickers and books and records. Where do all those profits go? Are these things being turned out for love of Jesus, or for love of the "almighty dollar"?

There is a lot of money in religion today. There is money in selling religious books—and some publishing houses are returning to religious books after once abandoning them for what they thought was more profitable. There is money in the occult and witchcraft, too, so some publishers go into that for the same reason.

Where does Jesus fit into all this?

God forbid that I should throw stones at any of the dedicated people who are distributing Christian books and music to so many corners of the earth. I salute them. I just don't want anyone to confuse God and mammon (money). Jesus warned long ago,

"Ye cannot serve God and mammon" (*see* Luke 16:13) and we still need that warning.

No, Jesus is no magic money tree. Instead of automatically showering money on us, He shows us what we could be doing for people in need—people like the *forgotten generation.*

12

The Forgotten Generation

Last Thanksgiving I was visiting some of the people in a home for the aged. One man I'll never forget. He was dressed up in a white shirt and tie, and his worn old trousers were pressed so neatly they looked as though they had just come from the dry cleaner. (I'd guess he had pressed them himself that morning.) "My son is coming to see me today," he told me proudly in his thin old voice.

All day long that poor old man sat in his room waiting for a son who never came. The last I saw of him that day, he was sitting there all by himself with a tray in his lap, chewing on a dry piece of turkey. He had been waiting all day, and at last he realized his son wasn't coming. There was such loneliness in his face! I could feel it for a long time afterward.

One of the worst things I see today is the way old people are treated. It starts early. By the time you reach forty you may be in trouble. Try getting a good job at that age or older! No way! Forty means you are over the hill as far as most jobs are concerned; the companies look for younger people they can start at lower pay.

If you are fortunate you will retire on a pension. A lot of people never get even a small one. A famous manufacturer closed his factory in one city and thousands of men who had worked there suddenly lost their jobs. Some of the workers were in their sixties, too old to get a job anywhere else. All of them were left with no pension, *nothing*—and one man would have retired in less than a year.

One of the worst things about the inflation that is galloping so fast these days is what it does to older people. The ones lucky enough to have small pensions find that every week their few dollars buy less and less. Some old people have to choose between food and fuel. On Christmas Eve of 1973 a ninety-three-year-old man and his wife were found frozen to death in Schenectady, New York. Four days before, the power company had turned off their electricity because they hadn't paid their last bill, and they couldn't start their furnace.

A lot of older people do not have enough money to buy bare essentials. Some live on little besides stale bread and cheap margarine. An old lady at a supermarket check-out counter found she didn't have enough money to pay for the few things in her arms, and she put back a can of cat food.

The check-out girl was sympathetic. "It's too bad," she smiled, "you won't be able to bring that to your cat."

"I don't have a cat," the elderly woman said. "That was for me."

Some old people are forced to live on pet food.

Frankly, I don't understand the way so many senior citizens are treated. From my earliest days I remember the love and honor and respect I used to see showered on the old. My Grandfather Ignacio lived in my childhood home, in spite of our big family, until he died. Mom was always fixing chicken soup for him—and other things he especially liked. All our elderly relatives were cared for in the same way.

In Puerto Rico when I was young, that was the way most old people were treated. They were loved and cherished and respected, and if an old person was neglected, everyone regarded it as a scandal and shame. People tell me it used to be the same way in the United States. Families had big houses and there was generally room somewhere for Grandma or Grandpa when either or both couldn't live alone any longer.

How different it is in so many places today! Houses aren't big enough anymore to hold an older relative, and the grandparents who live long enough to need care are often shunted off out of sight into nursing homes or other places for the aged. Modern children miss the great blessing of knowing their parents' parents, and they miss all the wisdom they could gain from this contact. Today's older generation misses the joy of entering into the life and growth of the younger generation.

When an elderly person chooses to live alone, that's a different matter. My own mother chooses to live with my niece in Las Piedras, Puerto Rico, but some of my brothers and their families live close by, and her children and grandchildren are always dropping in. My brother José Ramon lives in the house next to Mama and he keeps a watchful eye on her. My mother knows she is not neglected. She knows that any of us children would be glad to have her come and live with us anytime. During the summer months Mama sometimes comes to New York to visit. On those visits she spends one or two weeks with each of my brothers and my sister who live in New York, and each family fights to have her visit them first.

We have got to learn how to restore the honor and care we owe to the ones who loved us and sacrificed so much for us when we were young.

God expects that of us. He says, "Honour thy father and thy mother" (*see* Exodus 20:12) and He has never repealed that law. It is not honor to let an aged mother or father slowly starve—from lack of *either* food or affection—nor to hide them away in some institution and forget all about them.

Jesus tells us to love our neighbors as ourselves, and He does not say not to include our parents. And He set such a wonderful example Himself, for all time. Do you remember when He was dying, stretched out on that cross on Calvary? Nearly all the disciples had deserted Him at the end. One who stuck by Him right to the end was the disciple who loved Him so much, the Apostle John. Practically the only other one who dared to stand by Him at the cross, when everyone was ridiculing Jesus and spitting on Him, was His mother.

And while Jesus was dying there, bearing the sin of the whole world on His great shoulders, taking that awful burden on Himself, He was thinking about His mother.

Jesus didn't want His best friend to be left all alone and He didn't want His mother to be neglected. What a wonderful thing He did for both of them! He said to Mary, "Woman, behold thy son!" And to John, "Behold thy mother!" (*See* John 19: 26, 27.)

If Jesus could do that while He was dying the worst death the world has ever known, how can we neglect taking care of our own mothers and fathers?

Among Latins, old men and women are truly respected and honored. People admire their experience and wisdom and come to them for advice. In some of the so-called underprivileged countries, a child has a hard time when he's young, but as he gets older, things get better, until in old age he has the best, happiest time of his life. There is a lot of criticism about America's South, but I respect and admire the way most Southerners treat their older people, and that goes for both black and white.

Today many people practically idolize their children. Anything they want, they can have! Pain and suffering and problems we keep away from them—until they learn the hard way that there are such things. But the future they should anticipate with hope is often a time of dread, for even young children can sense the way most older people are treated. So life often ends in misery and depression and loneliness and sadness.

We reject old age today! Actors and actresses and the models who sell us products have to be young and exciting and wrinkle-free. We hide our old people out of sight. Why? Is it because the sight of the aged reminds us that *we too* must someday grow old and die? We've got to learn to be honest with ourselves and just and fair to the old.

What can we do for them?

We could see that the fixed incomes of the aged fluctuate in some way with inflation, so that their few dollars won't buy less and less.

We could reduce their taxes.

We could rethink our priorities. Education is certainly important for our children, but what would happen if every community slowed down on its tax increases for new buildings and other expenses for children's public education until more is done for the aged?

A number of churches have homes for the elderly, and that's good, but can we stop there? There are Christian ministries to the young, the poor, the minorities, and all kinds of special groups, but where is the ministry to the old? Who watches over their welfare, spiritual or physical?

How I wish I could challenge everyone who reads this book to start right now thinking and praying and *doing something about our forgotten generation.*

The fact that a person has had sixty-five or seventy or eighty birthdays should not mean that he or she has lost touch with life. I believe that most older people are just as pleased with Christmas and Easter observances, with birthday parties and picnics and good times as younger people. They like interest and attention and time and love just as much or more. And how often *no one* meets these needs.

In one community a number of young people were assigned specific older people for contact and help. Several teen-agers and oldsters became fast friends!

Some churches today require each committee or group to represent minority groups, the young, and so on. How about making sure they also represent the old?

One thing is for sure. Unless the Lord returns first, every one of us will one day be wrinkled and old. How will we feel then? Will we be able to look back over our lives with satisfaction, knowing we have given of our best for the generation that seemed old when we were young?

13

Before the Fall—Pride

I was invited to speak in a certain city in May. A week before the date, I sent Bill Rhodes, one of my staff members, to check on the arrangements.

"Find out what they've been doing to advertise the crusade," I asked Bill. "Also how many prayer chains have been set up for support. Check on the size of the auditorium, the lighting—you know, all those little things that are so important to our crusades."

Bill went, but when he reported back to me he looked so dejected I couldn't understand it. "What's the trouble, Bill?" I asked. "You look as though you're ready to write a new song:

I have the gloom, gloom, gloom, gloom
Down in my heart!

"I suppose so," Bill said with a sigh. "I just can't take any more of what I've been through."

Bill explained. When he had arrived at the scene of my coming crusade, Bill had been treated, he felt, like dirt. There were good plans under way, but every suggestion Bill made to improve them was rejected outright. The local crusade committee took a totally negative attitude toward everything Bill said; nothing could be added to or taken away from their plans—not even the smallest detail.

95

Result: I had to go to the crusade site earlier than I had planned, simply to do what the committee hadn't let Bill do. Miraculously, the instant I arrived, I felt as though I was being treated like God. I made exactly the same suggestions Bill had, but this time everyone outdid himself to do what I asked.

It was too much for me. Reluctantly I took one of the committee members aside and told him how I felt about all this. "You have shamed me," I told him, "that you would treat another Christian brother as you treated Bill. You treated him completely different from me. Yet Bill works for me; he came here as part of the crusade, part of me, and you rejected him!"

The man looked down. I think he was beginning to realize what he had done and what it would mean. For it was quite clear by now that the men of the crusade committee had been guilty of one of the worst sins of all—pride.

Pride! It is so dangerous because it is so hard to recognize. We treat some people like pieces of furniture, instead of persons, because we are so wrapped up in our own affairs that we never think of how the other person feels. We discriminate shamefully. We go out of our way to praise and please one person while we practically step on another.

Even our prayers can be soaked in pride. One man of prayer gave God 10 percent of his income, fasted often, and would no more have committed adultery than he would have missed church. In his prayers this man was likely to say: "I thank you, God, that I am not greedy, dishonest, or immoral, like everybody else" (*see* Luke 18: 9–14 TEV). But God never heard those spiritually proud statements. We know that is one kind of prayer which God will not answer because Jesus told us so in this parable of the Pharisee and the tax collector. Look it up and you will find that Jesus tells us that God will listen more readily to the humble sinner who turns to Him than to the religious person who is filled with pride.

Pride corrupted the world in the beginning. Adam and Eve wanted to be as wise as God, and they set themselves above Him, listening to the devil's false promises instead of God's clear commands. But pride was around long before the Fall! That *super-*

corruptor Satan started out as one of God's highest angels. Somewhere along the line Satan developed delusions of grandeur and coveted the throne of God for himself. His unchecked pride left God no choice: He had to banish to the bottomless abyss the devil and all the angels which got behind him. I wish they would stay there! One day they will be sealed up forever, but right now —as everyone who follows Jesus knows—those fallen spirits are at work night and day trying to get you and me into their wicked ranks. Since they cannot get to the Creator, they settle for His Creation or the part of Creation that most touches His heart— man!

Since God recently spoke to me in Ottawa, I have seen the sin of pride so often! In the *name-droppers,* for instance. A man may come up to me and say, "When I was talking to Billy Graham and Senator Stennis recently, I thought of something Pat Boone told me about how the Lord worked in the life of Maria von Trapp." God forgive me if I judge people like this wrongly, but I can't help being suspicious that for them I'm one more name to add to their list, so that they can tell the next person they meet, "As Nicky Cruz told me the other day. . . ."

And then there are the people who get in touch with me (I suspect) to make money. I am approached about so many money-making schemes, you wouldn't believe it. I've turned them down because I know if I started that route, at best I would end up living for money and what it can buy, and that's not what I've given my life to God to do.

It's all a form of the old, old appeal of pride—thinking of things instead of people, thinking of yourself instead of others, putting God last instead of first.

Pride is treating someone differently because he isn't *somebody*. Pride is asking, "What's in it for me?" instead of, "How can I serve the Lord in this situation?" Pride is an attitude—"I can't benefit from knowing that person, or from talking to him or spending my time with him—so I won't bother with him."

Pride is so widespread in the world today. The lust of the eyes and the flesh and the pride of life are waiting to trip you up at any time, and the only way to avoid those spiritual land mines is to ask God over and over to keep you straight and humble and dedicated to Him. So many people build their lives around pride. They spend so much time building themselves up, trying to create a false image, getting to know the right people, belonging to the right club—hoping this approach will give them the answers to their problems. It won't because it can't! Pride is one of the worst corruptors of all, and as I write these words I pray that the Lord will keep me from it, and save from it every person who reads these words.

Pride is such a sneaking temptation. You've heard of the fellow who was proud to say *he* wasn't proud! That's how tricky pride is. And it gets mixed up with so many other things. Nearly everyone could use more money or a nicer car or home and wants to be a success. The sin comes in when things like that become such a passion that we put them ahead of the things that are really important. And then we have to be the best politician, the most successful businessman, the finest athlete, the richest millionaire, the best singer in the choir, the hardest worker in the church! Yes, pride seeps into everything we do for the Lord, too, and we have to keep a constant watch against it.

So often in the churches, the poor family that comes to the Lord is overlooked while the banker, politician, or famous person who joins, is asked almost automatically to serve at the next election to the official board. And he may not have the spiritual background for this at all. Money counts for too much, even in the church! James asked, in effect, "Are you going to show more attention to the people of wealth and influence who may come to church than the poor and the really needy ones? The ones lowest down may rank highest in the eyes of God!" (*See* James 2:1–9.)

Our attitudes need changing and cleansing, so pride will not ruin all we do.

Even as I say this, I realize that it may look as though I'm up on a pedestal looking down on "the proud." I know how easy it is for pride to get into my own life. Let me try to be completely honest here. I know I take pride in myself and in the work God uses me to do. It seems to me only natural and right to take some degree of pride in accomplishment. I don't believe that kind of pride is wrong, if you keep in mind that you can't really accomplish anything without God's constant help. But if you forget His enabling, if you let pride *rule your life,* if you begin to think you're naturally better than somebody else—you're in deep trouble.

Let me make it clear what pride means to me. First of all, pride should not be confused with how you value yourself personally. The first thing that impressed me about the Lord was how He looks at every one of us as individuals. He loved *you* enough to give His life for you, and that means you're valuable! You can't get lost in the crowd. The Bible says that all the hairs of our heads are numbered. Think of it—every day some hair falls and new hair grows in, and the Lord knows all about what is happening! He *loves* us! If the Lord loves us, we should love ourselves and place real value on what we stand for.

I have been traveling extensively for almost ten years and I have to admit that the Lord has had to slap me down because of pride that sneaked into my life. I was preaching in Pittsburgh. I had grown aware of the uniqueness of my ministry, of how I had become something of an adult and teen-age idol. I knew how to present myself in a way that made people put me in their mental Hall of Fame. I had prayed before the meeting, but it had been a selfish prayer, more asking God to "Give me. . . ." than I like to remember. Everything went well in my meeting until the most important part of all, the altar call. At that point I began to choke and could hardly get out the words. I was humiliated.

After the meeting was over, when I returned to my hotel room, I felt that I had received a slap from the Lord. It was as if I had been in a rumble and lost the fight. I felt ashamed.

But I needed that rebuke. I learned that God can pop the balloons of our pride and cut us down to size.

As the Bible puts it so well, pride goes before a fall (*see* Proverbs 16:18 and 29:23).

And pride can corrupt your calling. That's what I want to tell you about next.

14

Don't Corrupt Your Calling

Soon after David Wilkerson brought me to Jesus, I went to Bible college in La Puente, California. After I graduated, the first job I got was in a restaurant in Oakland. I had a few months —five, to be exact—and then I would be off with my new bride, so in the meantime I got a job as a busboy. That's right, a busboy! I cleaned tables, swept floors, washed dishes. The restaurant was one of the nicest eating places in Oakland, right on Jack London Square. People with money, and many celebrities, came there to dine and drink. (Maybe I should put that the other way around, and say they *spent money like crazy and drank like fish.*)

The atmosphere was not exactly healthy, morally or spiritually, for a Christian right out of Bible college. It was certainly a challenge to everything I had learned and called for every scrap of spiritual protection I could find. I thank God that He was with me, because I knew this was where He wanted me to be for a while, even though deep in my heart I knew that He was calling me into a definite future ministry.

At the restaurant worked another busboy who was also from Puerto Rico. His name was Roberto. I discovered he was constantly watching me. Puerto Ricans are very emotional people and Roberto was no exception to the rule. Before long I learned exactly how he felt about me.

Often Roberto and I ate lunch together in a side room after

L.I.F.E. College Library
1100 Glendale Blvd.
Los Angeles, Calif. 90026

the main push at lunchtime was over and we could have a little breather. One day as I was thanking God for the food, Roberto started laughing.

"Why are you talking to yourself?" he asked.

I stopped in the middle of my prayer and I explained that I was thankful for everything Jesus gave me, and so I thanked Him for food and everything else. I said I knew Jesus personally, that He was right there with us, and I made it clear I was very serious about my faith.

Roberto sat there stunned. I knew he had been making fun of me before. To him it had been a funny sight to have someone talking to someone who wasn't there. The idea that Jesus was there in the room shook him up. Roberto didn't know what to say.

The next couple of days Roberto watched me constantly. Wherever I went in the restaurant, whatever I did, I could feel Roberto's eyes on me, and I knew he was thinking and wondering. I took Roberto to my heart in prayer, and I shared what I knew about Jesus whenever I had the chance. I told him about the old days of witchcraft and fear in Puerto Rico, and the gang days in New York, and what Christ had done for me—and was doing every day. Roberto looked and listened.

Only one week later Roberto came with me to church. At the close of the service, when the invitation was given to come forward and accept Christ, Roberto went forward and knelt down at the altar and gave his life to the Saviour.

That was just the beginning. Most Puerto Ricans have large families, and counting all his brothers and sisters there were at least fifteen in Roberto's. Through Roberto's newfound faith, every last member of his family, including his grandfather and grandmother, accepted Jesus.

Three days after Roberto's conversion I left my job as a busboy to begin my own ministry. At the same time, Roberto quit to enter Bible college. Today he is a minister of the Gospel, giving all his time and effort to bringing Jesus to others.

What a blessing Roberto brought me! No matter how unknown I was at the time, no matter how insignificant I might be in anyone's eyes—and to many of the people I served, I was just a robot, moving food and dishes—I knew I had done something eternally important. It didn't matter now what happened. I knew that God was in control, and that He would honor me if I honored Him. It didn't matter whether anyone else knew what happened. Lives had been changed, and would be changed, for the Lord. I came to that job a plain, straight Christian who loved Jesus. I was in the right place at the right time, and I left at the right time.

I began speaking to the Spanish-speaking churches in the area, and I found many hearts hungry for the Word. There were tremendous numbers of sincere people who listened, as Roberto had, to my simple message of Jesus and His love and power. The burden to share Him grew deeper and deeper within me. I became very happy in those years of growing and sharing, and I never questioned God.

And little by little I changed from a nobody to a somebody. God opened door after door, and the name Nicky Cruz became one which people started talking about.

When you become a "personality" it is easy to forget how your work began. How do you keep yourself humble when you see your name all over a city like a movie star's? How do you make the right decision when someone does something wrong to you, or forgive when you don't feel like forgiving? These are questions I never find easy to answer. Prayer is constantly needed so as not to fall into temptation and pride. It is so easy to lose the burden God gave you, to lose sight of your calling, to forget that the Lord has brought you so far. There is a deep need to come closer and closer to Jesus every day, and never to forget Him.

I have such beautiful memories, as I think back, of all Jesus has done for me. I think of all the friends who pray for me. I look for such people wherever I go. They are part of my life. Without them and Jesus I couldn't do a thing. I try not to forget these partners in my ministry and their love and prayers.

People often ask me, "Nicky, how did you get to where you are today?" It has not been *my* doing. Whatever I have done is a tribute to Jesus and my partners in prayer.

But I want to emphasize this. While I was attending Bible

college, I wanted to become a missionary in South America. It seemed like the natural thing to do, and what God would have me do. I knew Spanish, I was Spanish, I came from a Latin American country, so what else could God want me to do?

I announced my conclusion to the dean of the school, and I will always remember what he said:

> Nicky, the will of God is not always what we want, or even what we may be quite sure is right. The best way to fulfill the will of God in your life is to serve Him totally every day. God may want to send you to South America. He may want to keep you right here in California. I have an idea that He has a great ministry ahead for you. But I learned long ago that the Lord's ways are greater than our ways, and often far different from anything we can think or dream. Let it be the center of your ambition to give Him all your energy each day of your life, and He will take you where He wants you to go.

How true I have found those words of that wise man of God. I have made it my ambition to serve God to the best of my ability every day, day by day, and moment by moment, and God has done for me more than I could ask or think.

It is so easy to fail in this area. We tend to take our eyes off the sky and look at the mud below. No one should ever corrupt the value of the calling of God in his life. Neither should we limit it, or be tempted into fanaticism. We must learn to know ourselves and to know God, and as we make serving Him every day the center of our ambition, He takes care of the rest.

It is easy to dream of the green pastures on the other side of the fence. People write to me so often to the effect: "If only I didn't have this job (or this wife or husband or this problem) how I would love to serve the Lord as you are doing."

My dear friend, don't corrupt your calling. God has put you where you are just as He led me years ago to work as a busboy. If I hadn't been true to Him there, none of the other wonderful things that followed would have happened. Roberto wouldn't be bringing men and women and boys and girls to Jesus today, and so many opportunities for God would have gone right down the drain.

Happiness in hardship—what a blessing! I remember the tough times which David Wilkerson went through when he was first trying to get hold of us gang people in New York. So often he was down to his last dollar! But he never let the hardships stop the work he knew God had called him to do. I didn't know it in the beginning, but I know now that David had three very important things in his life that kept him from getting discouraged and quitting.

One was *faith*. Like the David in the Bible who killed the giant Goliath, David Wilkerson trusted that God would do His part if he did his. Sometimes I used to wonder why he prayed so much. Now I know that he kept his faith strong with much praying and reading the Bible. Another thing David Wilkerson had was a *positive attitude*. He expected to reach his goals, he never let negative ideas get the upper hand, he expected great things from God, and attempted great things for God. A third thing in David Wilkerson's life was his *relationship to his wife*, Gwen. She had the beautiful habit of helping him forward instead of pushing him down, and she was a real fellow worker with him in the Lord. So David Wilkerson didn't corrupt his calling!

(Let me add right here that one of the corruptors I often come across today is the attitude of the wife who does keep pushing her husband down. I don't think some women realize that they are doing this, but *they do it*—and their husbands know it! Please, ladies, be encouragers to your husbands, not discouragers. Remember that you are one of the biggest reasons behind whether your husband is a success or a failure, happy or depressed.)

I remember my own early experiences in Teen Challenge. In the beginning we did not have a car, and that first winter I walked through the snow to visit my old buddies from the gang. My salary was twenty-five dollars a week, and yet there was so much satisfaction from working in the ministry of Christ! My heart filled with thanksgiving every time a young man or woman was saved.

Have you heard of Sonny Arguinzoni? When he began his ministry in Los Angeles, he lived in one of those low-rent building projects where his life and the lives of his family were often in danger. Sonny didn't have enough money to pay the rent much of the time, or to buy food or clothes for his children. Once Sonny's assistant pastor went to preach in a church that wanted to know about the work, and they gave him a love offering. When they counted it they found it came to twenty dollars! Both Sonny and his assistant needed that money for rent, but Sonny gave it to his assistant.

Today Sonny Arguinzoni's ministry is unique in every way. It is one of the most outstanding examples of spiritual outreach in the whole Los Angeles area. The Drug Addicts' Church—Victory Temple, the women's home (some of the women have their children with them), the men's home, the ranch—these are all places where the Spirit of God is at work. I cry inside when I see Sonny preaching and leading this ministry. There are some who criticize Sonny and say, "He has it made!" I believe the critics are jealous of Sonny Arguinzoni's success. He is a success in every respect, but the critics don't know what it took when Sonny was starting his ministry.

Another man who has come through unbelievable hardship is Luis Rosario, the director of our Outreach center in Puerto Rico. Luis has a lovely home, neat and clean as can be. But there is not a wasted nickel in anything Luis and his wife do. They have never bought new furniture. Luis has taken things that were given to him and painted and repaired them until they look like new. This way he feels he is free from debt to work more freely for the Lord.

Luis is right. I do not believe that ministers should get in debt or that they should always be wanting what other people have. That's a good way to let Satan gain dominion over you! Luis has been faithful in his ministry, and faithful waiting on the Lord to supply every need, never questioning his calling. To me that is the mark of a healthy spiritual giant. To people like that I take off my hat. They can identify with suffering and need because they have experienced it themselves. Why shouldn't they enjoy success when it comes? And why shouldn't they find success in the Lord's good time?

I am hurt and concerned about the outlook of some Christians and even some ministers in relation to others who prosper. There is evident a sense of pessimism, cynicism, jealousy, and resentment when someone succeeds spiritually or financially. So many ask, "Why not me?" They forget that these successes were often happy and grateful and joyful people even when they didn't have so much. They took a positive attitude toward the little things, believing that the Lord can bless a little today as He blessed the fishes and the bread in Galilee. The successful ones who have come through difficulties take the attitude, "Now that I have it, I must be careful." The critics are often so negative they wouldn't be satisfied with anything. They forget to count their blessings and are always in the turmoil of dissatisfaction and complaining.

Don't corrupt your calling. Be content with the thing God has called you to do whether it's a big thing or a little thing. Praise Him for your opportunities, right where you are, right now.

15

Corruptor Number One

At this point you may be wondering why I haven't said something about one of the specific forms of corruption about which *you* are most concerned. I wish I had room! I could fill a book ten times the size of this one with just a few of the things that could be written about corruption and destruction, and I still wouldn't have done much more than scratch the surface. So let me see if we can't get down to basics.

When I was quite small, I can remember hoeing some weeds in my father's garden and thinking that I was doing a good job. I got rid of a whole row of weeds—at least I went down the row of beans and chopped off every weed in sight. When I got to the end of the row I stopped and looked back, pretty proud that all the weeds were gone. Then I noticed my father watching me. He came over to where I was leaning on my hoe and asked, "Are you finished, Nicky?"

"Sure!" I said. "Look, Father, the weeds are all gone!"

"No, Nicky," my father said. "Look." He knelt down in the garden and poked his finger into the ground. "See this root? As long as you leave the roots, the weeds will keep growing. It's not enough to chop off the tops. You must cut deep into the ground and kill the roots if you want to keep the weeds from growing."

So far in this book we have been chopping down some bad corruptors. But what about all the others? What about getting rid of corruption for good? How about killing the *root!*

Some people may think it just happens that there are so many corruptors in the world. They think it is human nature or an accident that so many good things are spoiled by so many bad things —pride, greed, violence, and all the rest. I say that if you see many plants of a weed growing close together, you know they come from the same root. And if you see the same kinds of corruption spoiling things in every part of the world over hundreds of years, they must grow out of one root.

To put it another way, when a number of women in Boston were all strangled in the same way, the police concluded that the murders were all committed by the same person. They were—by the Boston Strangler. When people all over the world are destroyed morally and spiritually in the same basic way, sensible people should conclude that the destruction must come from one source. The Bible says that source is the devil—the biggest corruptor of all times.

A lot of people get uptight if you mention Satan. That name may bring a mental picture of someone with horns, a tail, and a pitchfork, but I'm not talking about a fantasy. The devil is a reality.

To understand him, you've got to go back to the beginning. Originally, as many Bible passages show, Satan was one of the highest and most beautiful angels in heaven. He was close to God. He must have wanted to be bigger than God. And at some point before the earth was created, Satan swelled with pride. He conspired with other angels to try to overthrow God and take His throne. Naturally, the plot failed. When God saw the wicked pride in that powerful being, He cast him and the other evil angels clear out of heaven.

Satan had once been one of the most beautiful angels in heaven. His name in the beginning was Lucifer—angel of light. So when God made the world and planned for man to be happy in it and lead a beautiful life there, the devil was watching and waiting to spoil it all, just as he had tried to spoil heaven.

God took His time in separating the land from the water, creating the birds, the fish, the plants and trees, and He took just pride in everything He made. Finally He made human beings in

His own image, as the crowning glory of His work. Of all the creatures God ever made, only man was made in His image. This shows how highly He thought of mankind. When God had completed His creation, He looked upon it and said, "This is good!"

God created Adam from the dust of the earth and placed him in a situation where he could really make a difference. He learned to call everything by name—the cattle, the birds, and every beast (*see* Genesis 2:20). The first man was his own computer. God gave him the mind to acquire knowledge and the wisdom to do all this. And God had beautiful communication with Adam. There was fellowship all the time, especially in the evening, in the cool of the day when God walked through the Garden of Eden and talked with that man who is the ancestor of us all.

But God felt that man needed a companion. He put Adam to sleep and out of his side He took a rib and of it created a woman to be this companion. The two were very happy. God gave them His law and revelation to guide and inspire them. They had the privilege of doing whatever they wished. They could eat anything in Eden but one thing—God told them not to eat of the fruit of the tree of knowledge of good and evil.

Then the battle started! Satan never rests in peace. He is always planning, plotting, conspiring against God. Satan wanted to hurt God, and the best way to accomplish that was to get at the being of which God was most proud, and that was man. From that day, the witchcraft started. Satan himself entered a serpent that was in the garden. Never in history has there been another record of a serpent speaking, but this serpent talked to Eve and she replied.

Satan guessed that the woman in Eden was weak. (Men are generally considered the stronger, although in some ways women appear tougher than men.) But the devil knew that the best way to get at Adam was through Eve. And his first step was to inject his personality into her mind. He tried to give her the idea, "You think that God told you not to eat that fruit because doing that would make things go wrong. But I promise you, eat it and you'll be as intelligent as God. You'll be able to see yourself as you are —and you will know good and evil, just like God."

It was a low trick, half truth and half lies, like all of Satan's deceptions, but Eve fell for it, and Adam fell, and as a result all mankind fell. From that day forward death came into the world through sin.

Adam and Eve were deceived by the devil, but there was some truth in his deception. After that, they could really see themselves. Their eyes were opened and they saw their nakedness before each other and before God. They felt ashamed!

Although Adam and Eve discovered the form of the human body, there was nothing wrong with this discovery in itself, but in this case, Adam and Eve made the big mistake of letting pride take over. They let sin control them, they fell, and were cast out of the garden.

Men have never been satisfied. They are always wanting to *do their own thing*. Man wants to build his own kingdom and be his own god. The generations have proved that. There was a time when the people of God, the Israelites, were slaves in Egypt. God sent them a liberator when the people asked for someone to bring them out of bondage. And God found Moses to do it. Moses talked with God. He believed so strongly in his heavenly Father that he refused to compromise with sin. Moses was the kind of man which God could use, and Moses took the people out of slavery.

There was a festival—a celebration—when the Israelites had crossed the Red Sea. Festivals didn't start with Woodstock and Watkins Glen. Moses' sister Miriam took a tambourine and danced. Everyone was dancing and happy. There were so many beautiful feelings resulting from this freedom, from no longer living in fear and captivity. The festival went on while Moses went up into Mount Sinai to pray and to receive the Lord's guidance. He was there many days, and while he was gone, Satan got busy again. This time he injected into the people's minds a dissatisfaction with their leader and he gave them the idea that they should have a god they could see and touch. So when Moses finally came down from the mountain with the Ten Commandments, the people were dancing in lust and worshiping an idol they had made with their own hands. Moses could not endure this. He became so indignant that he smashed the Commandments, engraved on stone tablets by God Himself (*see* Exodus 32: 1–19).

A number of times after that, Satan filled the people's minds with rebellion, discontent, grumbling, criticism, and unbelief. Once this brought a plague of serpents among them. At another time, God would have destroyed them all had not Moses interceded to win their forgiveness by God. Again and again, the Israelites went their own way instead of God's and it was only His patience and love which kept them from destroying themselves.

For centuries after, there was revealed the same story of sin, punishment, and finally repentance and deliverance. The famous Samson was known not only for his superhuman strength, but for his moral weakness. Delilah was one of the women whom Samson loved. She was paid a high price to learn from her lover the secret of his great strength. While he was sleeping, Delilah cut Samson's hair and turned him over to the Israelites' enemies, the Philistines, who gouged out his eyes and put him in prison. During a great pagan festival, Samson was brought out of prison in chains to amuse the Philistines in the temple of their god Dagon. At that moment, this tragic hero prayed for the restoration of his lost strength and pulled down the temple. It is written that those Samson killed in his death were more than all the enemies he had killed in his lifetime (*see* Judges 16). Once again, Satan almost seemed to get the best of God's people, but at the last moment, God's side won the final victory.

On another occasion, God used a woman named Deborah to deliver His people from their enemies. She was a prophetess and judge with unusual talents for executive and military leadership. Deborah commanded the Hebrew general Barak to gather his troops and fight the opposition Canaanites. Reluctantly, Barak carried out his mission with Deborah at his side and the enemy was routed (*see* Judges 4).

The people asked God to give them a judge and prophet, and

He gave them Samuel, one of the great men of God. Samuel was used by God to tell the old priest Eli that his house would be punished for the sins he had permitted his sons to commit (*see* 1 Samuel 3:11–18).

Still dissatisfied and envious of the kings who led other nations, the Israelites asked God for a king of their own. This hurt God, for He had been more than a king to His people, but He answered their demand. Their first king was Saul, a handsome, tall, egocentric, and worldly man who "spelled trouble" early in his reign. Saul was dependent on Samuel at first. He was confused and didn't know how to rule as a king and soon refused Samuel's help when the prophet tried to counsel him. After Samuel died, Saul went to a witch and tried to communicate with the departed prophet (*see* 1 Samuel 28:7–19). This was one of the early recorded instances of alleged communication with the dead. The devil must have laughed with much glee as Saul was deluded into seeking false ways out of his difficulties.

Then God gave to the people—David, a beautiful man and king. He was human and made many mistakes, but God loved him because he was sincere and honest. He didn't try to hide anything. When David saw the lovely Bathsheba bathing, he was so overpowered with desire that he sent for her and eliminated her husband by putting him on the front lines of the army, where he was killed in battle. Soon Bathsheba bore David's illegitimate child. But David didn't try to cover up his sin permanently. He wept many bitter tears over this tragic affair, and when he turned to God in true repentance, God forgave as He always does those who honestly turn to Him (*see* 2 Samuel 12:13).

There were both good and bad kings after that, but the people got tired of all of them and asked God again for a prophet. So He sent them not one prophet, but a number of them. Usually these men of God—Isaiah, Jeremiah, and others—were rejected and sometimes killed by the people, who did not really want to hear what God had to tell them. When Isaiah began to preach the truth and tried to bring the people together, they turned against him and according to ancient legend, this great prophet was finally sawn in half.

The last great prophet—the man who closed the Old Testament age and ushered in the age of Christ—was John the Baptist. John proclaimed His Coming and His Kingdom and really preached the Word of God! But what happened when he criticized the personal life of Herod Antipas, the head of the government? King Herod was committing adultery with his brother's wife, Herodias, and John had the guts to preach against that illicit passion. Herod was disturbed, but since he was somewhat in awe of the Baptist was not sure what to do. So furious was Herodias, however, that she searched for revenge through her daughter Salome. When Herod so admired her dancing that he promised her anything she wished, Salome, coached by Herodias, asked for the head of John the Baptist (*see* Mark 6: 17–28). So Satan managed to get rid of that prophet, too.

Give me! All through history, inspired by Satan, people have been asking God, "Give me, give me, give me." And God, the long-suffering, patient One, has been giving, giving, giving—and time after time Satan has laughed, because God seemed to be playing into his hands. Satan must have thought many a time, "Now, God, I've got You."

At last God had given men everything possible—His best gifts, His best servants. There was only One left for Him to give—His only Son, Jesus. God did not hold back His last, dearest possession. He saw the opportunity to save mankind, and so He sent Jesus to earth. The Saviour came willingly, eager to show what it is like for God to live on earth. He healed the sickness and wounds of many who lived in poverty and who had been falsely led by the wrong guidance, the wrong religion, into a wrong way of living.

When Jesus came to earth, the devil must have rubbed his hands and cried, "I've got You now, God! I'm going to hurt You real bad. I'm going to put the whole world out of balance. *I'm going to let You see Your Son tortured to death on a cross.*" When that happened, God found it unbearable to look on the sight. He had to turn His face away—He couldn't watch His Son going through that agony. There was the torture of the nails and the suffering and the physical exhaustion, but on top of all these, there was the pain that was even worse—the bearing on His body of the sins of the whole world. Jesus died that slow, horrible death for your sins and mine.

When Jesus hung on the cross He prayed, "Father, forgive them; for they know not what they do" (Luke 23:34). And He was so concerned about His disciples and His mother (*see* John 19:26, 27). Here we see Jesus' great compassion for man. He saw that His disciples were going through a time of anguish and loneliness. That was why He had been so concerned to promise them the Holy Spirit (*see* John 14:16–20). The Spirit would be another Friend and Comforter. He would strengthen them and give them courage and power. Without the Holy Spirit, we are as weak as kittens—with Him, we are stronger than lions.

We should be so grateful to Jesus for sending the Holy Spirit! And for going away to prepare a place for us, and promising to return (*see* John 14:3). I definitely believe in the Second Coming of our Lord Jesus Christ. Jesus explained it, the Bible says it, and I believe in Jesus and the Book.

While Jesus was dying, the devil must have been thinking, "Now I'm going to take over. I'll be able to rule the whole earth!" But all his plans backfired. For three days it looked as though Satan had beaten God. But on the third day Christ returned from the dead. The Resurrection proved that God lives and that Jesus is eternal, and that the devil can't win unless we let him. Death was conquered right there when Jesus rose.

Without the Resurrection, there would be no need to be a Christian. Any old religion would do! The real answer to Buddhism and all the other cults and superstitions is *Jesus.* Jesus Christ is greater than any false god. He came from the One God, He *is* God, and His Resurrection proves it.

With the Holy Spirit, we have God's best Gift in our daily personal lives. Before He left this earth, Jesus looked ahead and saw that His disciples would need divine power. So He instructed them on how to receive the Holy Spirit (*see* Acts 1:4–8). God and Jesus were way ahead of the devil. Satan was counting on getting rid of Jesus, but he couldn't have guessed that Jesus would return from the dead, and he never could have imagined what the Spirit would do.

We need the Spirit of God to live a full, powerful Christian life. Remember that the devil always tries to attack God through man—through you and me. That is his psychology and his technique. But, praise God!—with the protection of the Holy Spirit, he can't hurt us. With the Spirit's aid we can have complete communication with God. Through Jesus Christ we can talk with God—go straight to God to learn His will. We don't need anyone to intervene between God and ourselves. We can go into a corner, or any other place, and we can have this wonderful relationship with Jesus.

That is why I am so happy that Jesus took over after man sinned. Right at the beginning, back in Eden, God foretold that there would always be war between man and the serpent. But He promised that the serpent would bruise the heel of the woman's seed—and "it shall bruise thy head" (*see* Genesis 3:15). It happened! Satan struck at the seed of the woman—Jesus—and He stepped right on the serpent's head. Everything the devil tried to do backfired.

Jesus won!

16

Meet My Psychiatrist

Psychiatry is a big thing today. Among the jet set, it is as fashionable to be analyzed as it is to have your children's teeth straightened.

But I want to say right out: Medicine is a very good thing, a gift from God that we should all be thankful for. However, psychiatry doesn't have all the answers.

Not long ago the evening news program in one large state told a story tragic enough to wring tears from a stone. A psychiatrist who had been feeling very depressed left his office, went home, took a gun and murdered his wife and his sixteen-year-old daughter. The telecast ended with the camera zooming in on that teenage girl's room. Millions of viewers saw her bullet-riddled body slumped on the floor in a pool of blood. Then the camera moved to the book that had fallen from her hands. It moved close-up, so everyone could see the words on the cover: THE LONELY NOW —NICKY CRUZ.

How thankful I was that the young girl knew the Physician with the real power to heal.

As you know if you've read my other books, when I was president of the Mau Maus and the judge turned me over to the court psychologist, that expert failed. He tried hard to figure out what made me a gang leader, but I don't think he ever got near the real truth. So he finally gave up and told me I was doomed.

119

I know of some psychiatrists who solve one problem by creating another. One man struggling with sex temptations was advised to do whatever he felt like doing. Another man was so depressed he had the urge to throw himself in front of a train. He went to a psychiatrist who told him he ought to visit a prostitute. I say such advice is dead wrong.

In the last few years a number of psychiatrists have admitted having sex relations with their patients. After four women got involved in this way and then were abandoned by their psychiatrist-lover, one tried to commit suicide, two went into a deep state of mental depression, and the husband of a fourth patient killed himself after he discovered what his wife had been doing. Some therapy!

Dr. E. Fuller Torrey of the National Institute of Mental Health says that psychiatrists are in many ways like witch doctors. In his recent book, *The Mind Game*, Dr. Torrey says that both psychiatrists and witch doctors depend a lot on the patient's confidence and faith, both build up that confidence by projecting an image of expert ability, and both get cures in their own cultures which neither one could accomplish in the other's culture. What the psychiatrist achieves with his diploma, according to Dr. Torrey, the witch doctor achieves by rattling his gourd.

Even so, a *good* psychiatrist can help a lot of people. He listens to you—and in these days it's hard to find somebody who will simply listen to what you want to say. He accepts you as you are, not as you could or should be. He helps you sort out your feelings and problems. He helps you understand them. He helps you accept yourself, and your situation in life, and the people with whom you have to live or work. He gives you a new perspective on things. At best, your psychiatrist helps you move up to a better level of existence. He helps you make the best of yourself and your circumstances.

I'd like to introduce you to my own Psychiatrist. The One I have always listens to me. I can get an appointment with Him any time of the day or night. After an hour with Him I'm never told, "The time is up. Come again next week." My Psychiatrist always listens for as long as I want.

He accepts me. He knows all my weaknesses and mistakes, but no matter what I do, He never turns me off. He is never threatened by what I say or feel.

And He leads me to more than understanding. He does more than help me make the best of things. He makes me into a better person, able for anything. He does more than that. Sometimes He changes my circumstances, so the problems I was trying to cope with simply disappear.

Other psychiatrists charge fees that are out of sight for a good many people. My Psychiatrist never charges a cent.

A psychiatrist is a healer of the mind and spirit. My Psychiatrist is the Great Physician. Unlike some medical doctors, He has no hopeless cases; He never fails.

Soon after I found God at that amazing meeting David Wilkerson had in the St. Nicholas Arena years ago, I turned myself in to the police. I found myself standing before the same judge who had sentenced me before. He asked, "What are you doing here?"

"Your honor," I said, "about three days ago I gave my life to Jesus."

The judge's jaw fell open. He looked as though he was trying to figure out what I was saying but couldn't comprehend it. Obviously he couldn't believe it. All he seemed to be able to say was: *"What?"*

I said, "Your honor, about three days ago I gave my life to Jesus."

The judge said, "Sit down and wait right here."

I waited there in the courtroom for about forty-five minutes, wondering what was happening. The judge had disappeared into his chambers. I discovered later that the judge had telephoned the court psychologist who had said to me only a few weeks before, "Nicky, you're doomed. There's no hope for you."

About the time I felt like getting away from that courtroom as far as I could possibly get, the court psychologist walked in. I jumped to my feet.

"Doc," I said, "do you remember what you said to me the last time I saw you?"

"Yes, I remember."

"I've got good news for you, man! Three days ago I turned my life over to Jesus. I don't know too much about this Jesus stuff yet, but I can tell you one thing. I've never been so happy in my life as I have been for the last three days. I've been reading this Bible I have here. Listen to this!"

I opened my Bible to the first page and I read the whole first chapter of Genesis to the psychologist. When I got to the end of the chapter and stopped, he said: "Nicky, that's beautiful. I hope you make it."

The court psychologist, meant well. He had done his best. But he had to give up when it came to changing my life. He couldn't touch what the Great Psychiatrist did for me—in an instant!

And still does for me.

A good psychiatrist may be able to do one thing for you. Whatever your problem is, depression or marriage difficulties or something else, he may help you solve it. But then he turns you loose and that's the end.

Jesus never turns you loose. He is *a very present help,* as David knew (*see* Psalms 46:1).

Jesus didn't just lift me out of my troubles and then turn me loose. I need Him all the time—and He's there every time I need help.

I had a rough time writing *Satan on the Loose.* When I decided to write that book, I knew something about what I was going to be up against. I had watched my father, a witch doctor all his life, face all the powers of the demonic world when he decided to become a Christian. I knew how viciously those powers were still attacking my mother, a medium until she, too, became a Christian. Before writing that book I had been like a freed prisoner of war. Christ had redeemed me from captivity to Satan, and I had worked with Him to redeem other captives.

But in *Satan on the Loose* I was attacking Satan directly, exposing his sneaky plans to win the world completely to his horrible domination, and I knew that he was going to use every trick in his book against me.

He did.

When I started writing *Satan on the Loose*, I learned what it means to have the gates of hell wide open and feel the breath of Satan blowing in your face. I knew I would need superhuman power to face that ancient enemy—but I felt my energy drained away before I could get in my first blow. You know how sometimes you jump out of bed eager to start a new day? Well, the first morning after I started working on that book, I woke up exhausted. It was as though I could barely pull on my shoes—or open the Bible—or pray. God seemed a million miles away. I didn't feel like doing a thing.

Gloria, always very sensitive to my spiritual needs, asked, "What's wrong, Nicky?"

And I didn't even feel like telling her. I felt lost in a spiritual fog, and it seemed as though there was no way to get out. I was drained of energy and even of hope.

For eight months, while I plodded ahead with *Satan on the Loose*, I felt as though I was in one of those nightmares where you try to move and cannot. Once, when I was a boy in Puerto Rico, I dreamed I was Tarzan of the Apes. I dreamed that a gigantic jungle cat was in a tree over my head, crouched ready to spring at me—and I was frozen like a statue, unable to make a single move. Well, it was like that for eight months while I wrote *Satan on the Loose*. I felt like a powerless pygmy in the grip of a supernaturally strong, giant enemy.

I knew that anyone who gets into witchcraft or the occult has to be on guard against attacks on his mind and his sanity. When I felt so depressed, and I couldn't seem to find any way out, I wondered if Satan was winning his battle against my mind. I felt that I was getting into depths where Gloria couldn't help me, where no one on earth could help.

Outwardly I think I appeared happy and normal to most

people. But deep inside I was sad and depressed and I felt an incredible demonic weight on my soul. Sometimes I found myself sitting for hours, looking out the window, seeing nothing of the bright world outside but envisioning the darkness and hopelessness of the world of Satan. It was a weight and a feeling so powerful that I couldn't seem to find any way on earth to shake it off!

I kept wondering, *Why do I feel this way?* I searched my memory. It was real turmoil—I knew something was wrong with my spiritual life, but I just couldn't seem to find the cause—or the cure. The awful darkness seemed to be blotting out everything I should have known. I felt as though I was in a pitch-dark room at midnight with no way to find a light. I couldn't put my finger on what was wrong.

As those periods of depression and blackness swept over me and I stared out the window, I struggled against powers and forces that I could feel almost physically. I tried to pray, but it seemed like too great an effort even to call to God for help.

Then the Great Psychiatrist came to my rescue. Out of nowhere came the words: "Ask, and it shall be given you; seek, and ye shall find . . ." (Matthew 7:7). It was like a lifeline flung to someone drowning! I cried out in my heart: "Jesus, help me!"

And the miracle happened. Like the sun burning through fog, the Light of the World cut through the darkness and drove it back. My half-frozen heart began to warm in that wonderful sunlight. Joy and hope flooded through my being, and I knew that once more Satan was on the run.

One of my sessions with the Great Psychiatrist was while I was driving down the Los Angeles Freeway in 1966. I had just finished a youth crusade in Santa Ana. Three thousand people had listened to my testimony. When I invited them to accept my Saviour, hundreds crowded forward. It was thrilling for me, Nicky Cruz, once a gang leader, to be used that way by the Lord!

I thought of the European tour I had taken the year before. There had been some fabulous crusades in some of the biggest cities in Europe. London was especially fascinating. There I spoke in the great Royal Albert Hall. All around me, filling the arena in front of the speaker's platform and in tier upon tier filling that enormous building, the youngsters and oldsters of London listened to the message. There were girls in mini-mini-skirts, young gentlemen with long wavy hair and ruffled shirts who looked as though they had stepped out of the eighteenth century, and tough-looking molls and skinheads who were probably as much at home on the streets of London as I used to be on the streets of New York. When these young people came forward to accept Christ, I knew He was using me in ways that I never would have dreamed possible a few years before.

There was a feeling of excitement and anticipation before each of those meetings. When I spoke, I held nothing back. I lived all over again my desperate life of crime in the gangs, my discovery of Christ, my new life since. As those seeking Christ knelt under the hot glare of the overhead lights, I could feel the cool wind of the Spirit of God moving in their hearts, soothing their feverish spirits and implanting His new life within them. Communicating Jesus in this way was one of the most exalting experiences I have ever had.

Now, at Santa Ana, the same thing had happened all over again. Members of the runaway generation by the dozens were coming Home, finding the peace and security they had been searching for so desperately, in their Father's loving arms.

But going back over these scenes of triumph as I drove my Pontiac down the Los Angeles Freeway brought me some very mixed emotions. In a way it had been a thrilling thing to be able to lead so many young people to Christ. But I took no pride in my shameful past. There may be individuals who glory in violence or blood. It may well be that many youngsters who come to my meetings get a vicarious thrill out of hearing the details of the bloodshed and lust and anarchy that were once part of my life.

I don't. The fact is that it is very painful for me to talk about the muggings and murders and robberies and gang fights in my past. For me, preaching is harder than any of those gang battles. Whenever I step into a pulpit, or onto an evangelistic platform, I sense the cosmic conflict that is really taking place.

I know that Jesus is there, looking at all those people with His infinite love for every last one of them and longing to bring them to Himself. And I know that Satan is there too, desperate to keep all those thousands in his own clutches, ready to try anything to prevent them from turning to Christ. I can practically see Christ on one side, the devil on the other, struggling for the eternal soul of each person there. And I realize that what I say can tip the balance toward heaven or hell!

Realizing all that, I can't rattle off my life story like a salesman's spiel. I feel that I have to put everything I've got into it, and so I live all over again those moments of crime and lawlessness that are now so shameful for me to think about. If you think that isn't hard, ask yourself this question: How would you feel if you were asked to reveal in public all the lies and wrong desires and shameful things in your own past life? How would you like to do this, not once, but over and over again?

All these things crowded through my mind as I drove down the freeway toward the home I then had in Los Angeles. I implored:

> Lord, do I have to go through these experiences time after time? I thank You that I can identify with the sins and the problems of so many young people. You know how I rejoice that I can share Your vibrations of truth and freedom. I praise Your name that You can use me so often to bring so many young people to You. But it's such agony to live through some of these things, over and over! Do I have to keep doing it night after night, week after week? Isn't there some other way? Lord, You know I won't put on an act to play with people's emotions. You know that I can't be a robot, saying something I don't feel. When I tell what You did for me, I have to do it honestly, with all my feelings. You know it hurts because I do give myself 100 percent!

I felt torn apart. I wept from a broken heart. As I drove along the crowded freeway, tears kept filling my eyes.

All of a sudden I found myself almost fighting with the Lord. I was hurt. "Lord," I sobbed, "do people come to my meetings to find You, or do they come just to see a real live gang leader? Is this what You want of me, to become a public spectacle?"

For half an hour I poured out my heart.

Then the answer came.

Suddenly I felt a chill. I knew that Someone was there in the Pontiac with me. I became ashamed of the way I had been talking to Him. I knew He deserved every shred of my love and respect, and I'd been talking to Him like a teacher scolding a bad student.

I felt the Great Psychiatrist close to me.

Jesus spoke. It wasn't an audible voice. It was simply the Son of God speaking in my heart, in His quiet, beautiful way:

Nicky, this is why I picked you up out of the streets of New York. This is why I cleansed you and gave you new life. It is that you may share it with others. That you may tell everyone, good or bad, dirty or clean, wise or foolish, about Me. I know your feelings. Do not feel sorry for yourself. Do not rebel against what I ask you to do. Rejoice that you can be My witness at such a time as this.

I knew the Great Psychiatrist had heard all my questions, understood my agony, knew my rebellion. I knew that He had borne the torment with me, that He had accepted it into Himself and cleansed and forgiven and healed my hurts.

These words leaped into my mind:

I can do all things through Christ which strengtheneth me.

Philippians 4:13

My grace is sufficient for thee; for my strength is made perfect in weakness. Most gladly therefore will I rather glory in my infirmities, that the power of Christ may rest upon me.

2 Corinthians 12:9

The Lord knows that I cannot go into a pulpit without giving myself completely. He knows that when I speak it is a real experience for me. And because He knows my weakness, He goes into the pulpit with me, and truly His strength is perfected in my weakness.

I cannot understand how anyone can speak from a pulpit without Jesus. How can anyone speak about Him if He is not real to the speaker at that moment?

Once I sat in an airplane next to a man with a clerical collar. He was interested in my work, he said, because he believed in a relevant Gospel. But when I talked about Christ he moved slightly away from me and looked at me as though I were deranged. He didn't seem to have any idea of what it is like to have Jesus in the pulpit beside you. He didn't understand me, and I couldn't understand him.

I'm thankful that my Saviour did not save me and then forget about me. He keeps on saving me, from myself and from all kinds of impossible situations. I can do anything I have to do through Him.

It still tears me up to tell about my old life. But the Great Physician heals the wounds. I'm still aware that many of my listeners may be there for the thrill of blood and lust. But if Christ can use it all for His glory, I'm content.

I still worry that Nicky Cruz may be exalted instead of Jesus Christ. I want to ask you who read this to pray that He will always be the one I praise. But I realize now that as long as I trust Him, He can keep me in the right place. Now, with Paul, *I am sure that God who began the good work . . . will keep right on* helping me grow in His grace (*see* Philippians 1:6 LB).

I'm sure that as long as I live, I'll have problems. But I also know this: *With Jesus as my Psychiatrist, I'm ready for anything.*

17

Straight Is Beautiful

These days, if you don't smoke grass you may feel like a freak. Well, let me tell you that the *real* freaks are the acid freaks and the pot smokers and the troublemakers. They are the ones who get the headlines. The drug addicts, the revolutionaries, the protesters, the crooks, the heavies, the kidnappers, the killers —they're the ones that make the news. But the straights and the squares—the people who build up instead of tearing down, the ones who hold things together, who quietly go about their business doing good things—these are the people who really count. Freakiness and crookedness get talked about, but *straight is beautiful.*

I've seen that so often. Frank wanted to make a career in business and politics. When he started working for a chain of supermarkets he advanced fast, but the work just didn't satisfy him. In his heart he knew he was going to have to do more in life than make money. He came to work on my staff, and there he met Elizabeth.

Elizabeth had been brought up in a church in Indiana. But she was not content with just supporting her church. She wanted to find some Christian action, so she too found her way to the headquarters of Nicky Cruz Outreach. When Elizabeth met Frank, it didn't take long for the two to discover that they both had the same deep desire to go all out for Christ. Between them they have been a tremendous help in my work. And both Frank and Elizabeth will testify that nothing is more exciting than such 100 percent service.

It is a beautiful thing to see Jesus take someone who has been wrecked from drug abuse, or heading straight downhill in some other way, and change him totally. But I believe we often forget that the same power of Christ is often at work in Christians who have long lived quiet, peaceful lives, like Frank and Elizabeth. The same miracle of new birth has happened to them! When a caterpillar turns into a butterfly, it's a miracle of nature. But the same power of God is at work when a flower unfolds from an unpretentious little bud.

The change of personality, habits, and character is so evident when a *freak* of some kind is converted that the salvation of a *straight* may look like a lesser miracle. But if that's the way we look at it, we are wrong. For then, not only are we belittling Christ's omnipotent work, but we are downgrading those whose confession of Christ is just as real and just as life-changing as anyone's, though perhaps not quite so dramatic.

The change in my own life, from ghetto gang leader to evangelist and youth worker, along with many experiences since and many observations of American young people, has made me keenly aware of that misconception.

I have seen so many young people, eyes aglow, clamor to a stage to shake hands or get the autograph of Nicky Cruz. Some of these youngsters will not listen for five minutes to a parent or pastor or Sunday-school teacher talk about spiritual things. Yet they will stand in line for an hour, sit on the floor for two hours, and wait backstage for an hour more, just to have me sign my name in a book.

I know why some of this happens. A good many young people feel: "You've been there, Nicky. You know what I'm facing. You know what life is like for someone my age." There's truth in that. The Apostle Paul gave his testimony time after time, for the benefit of those who could identify with him. I've given my own testimony many times in my talks and my books. Thousands of people have told me that through my life story they saw themselves and their need for Christ. Yet I shudder at the thought that anyone's past experiences are glorified more than the Lord who brought about those experiences.

Perhaps, as I have been told so often, it is better for young people to have a Christian hero than some other kind. The fact is, this is a generation without heroes. So many of the inspiring figures of past years are now dead or gone from center stage. The astronauts were popular for a time, but how many people even knew the last team of astronauts was in outer space? Political heroes have turned out in so many cases to be frauds and phonies. Who can anyone look up to? But I don't want to be idolized. I will feel uneasy until I know that all the credit for changing a life like mine goes to Christ and His power and glory.

The One to look up to is not on earth but above. The Bible tells us to continue *looking unto Jesus the author and finisher of our faith* . . . (Hebrews 12:2). He is the One who saved us and will keep us going to the end!

The freaks and heavies—where are they now? I'll tell you where they are. Some of them are dead. Many more than I like to think about are buried from New York to Miami to Los Angeles, dead from drug overdoses, suicide, disease, or run-ins with the law. Some are behind bars for committing horrible crimes. Some have syphilis and other diseases. Some have suffered irreversible damage to the mind. Some are homosexuals. Some have turned to witchcraft and the occult. Others are lost in religions that they think will give them peace, although they will never find it without the Prince of Peace.

"I've got to find my identity," one young woman told me on the way from her parents' home to a New Mexico commune. Identity! Today you could hardly tell her from thousands of other young women like her—old before their time, worn and battered by life, the sparkle gone from their eyes, about as attractive as old shoes.

Come with me to a hippies' hangout in a midwestern town. A lot of them look like vegetables. They just aren't functioning anymore. They go through the motions of living, but they are zombies—dead on their feet, their souls are gone and they don't even know something is missing. Here's a gang of them sitting in a circle in this decrepit old house where they live. They pass a stick of marijuana around the circle and think they're having fun. No way! All of them look half-dead-to-the-world. This is being together? Where is the excitement, the joy?

Get me straight—it takes guts to stay away from situations like that and to know how to say *no!* Joseph worked for a man with a lot of money and a beautiful wife. One day while Joseph was alone in the house with his employer's wife, she tried to get him to go to bed with her. Joseph had the guts to say no. He just went on about his work trying to ignore her invitation for two reasons. One: He knew it wouldn't be fair to his employer. Two: He knew it would be a sin against God.

But Joseph's temptation, like most temptations, didn't go away. The woman kept trying to seduce the young man, and when he wouldn't give in she got angry. She waited until there was no one around and then she made a last try. "Come to bed with me," she whispered in Joseph's ear as she tried to pull him into her bed. Joseph managed to flee from her but the woman held on to his jacket, and when her husband got home she got her revenge.

"Look at what that Hebrew servant you like so much tried to do!" she screamed, waving the jacket in her husband's face. "While you were gone he came into my bedroom and tried to rape me, and when I screamed he ran away and left his jacket behind!"

The husband was so angry that Joseph went to prison—but the Lord was with him. The whole story is in your Bible, Genesis 39. Joseph had guts! He always stuck to his principles, and eventually, even though he was in a foreign land, he rose to the second-highest position in the government of Egypt, and when hard times came along he saved his people and his own family from starving.

Be proud of who you are, and be yourself. Stand for your principles even when it is hard.

I begin laughing when I see people who want to look like heavies. On a plane, I watched a lady who must have been well over fifty years old, strutting around in a tight sweater, dark glasses, and a miniskirt. She went around calling everybody "Honey" and she seemed to be trying to act like a starlet. I noticed that even when this woman crossed her legs, nobody seemed to be turned on. The fact is, people laughed at her. Young people are not at all the only ones with hang-ups. Corruption is in no way limited to teen-agers. Whatever your age, you can *choose* whatever you want to be: heavy or straight. And you will find if you choose to be straight, the pay is better. Your riches will be things money can't buy and nothing can take away, ever.

There are so many straight people whose lives show so clearly how completely Christ *does* save and keep! Take Park Tucker, brought up in the coal mines of Wilkes-Barre, Pennsylvania. By the time he was twenty-two, he was an old hand in the mines. He was working a quarter of a mile under the ground when the mine caved in. Two of his friends were killed instantly. A huge rock snapped Park's left arm, and with other rocks piling up around him, Park made God a promise: "If You save my life, I'll give it all to You."

When the rescuers got through the cave-in, they found him the only man still alive. He had to spend the next year in a hospital, but Park Tucker came through—and kept his promise. He went back to grade school—a giant among small children. He went through high school and college, struggling every minute, working his way. He got through and became a minister and then a chaplain in the federal penitentiary in Atlanta, Georgia. There he brought Christ to thousands of convicted prisoners.

You hear so much today about corrupt politicians, it's easy to get the idea that everyone is a crook. Everyone isn't! Look at Orrin G. Judd, a federal judge who often works sixty hours a week. When he learned of complaints against a home for retarded children, he visited it himself and ordered sweeping changes in its administration. Judge Judd is a Christian, active in his church and the American Bible Society. He, too, proves that straight is beautiful.

Take Kenneth Taylor. I'm pretty sure that at no time in his life would he have come any closer to experimenting with drugs or other freaky experiences than jumping into a pit of cobras. For a number of years he was an editor for Moody Press, writing Christian books in his spare time and raising a family. A straight, ordinary Christian!

One day during family devotions Ken realized that his children weren't getting much from the reading of the Bible, with all its "thees" and "thous." On the train to work he started putting the Bible into language his children could better understand. They liked it, and after he had rephrased the Epistles of Paul, Ken Taylor tried it on a publisher. And another. And another. Every single publisher turned it down. "What do we need of one more translation of the Bible?" they asked. "There are more than enough already!"

Taylor took his life's savings out of the bank, borrowed some more money, and printed his own *Living Letters.* He got a few orders. Taylor printed more copies and rephrased more of the Bible. Before long the work was taking so much time he resigned his editorial job and put all his efforts into what is now *The Living Bible*—one of the most successful, best-selling versions of the Bible since the *King James Version.*

The next time you open *The Living Bible,* thank God for straight, "ordinary" Christians like Kenneth Taylor, whose most dramatic experiences are simply doing the marvelous things to which God leads them. The world is full of people like that— and the most exciting, most satisfying thing you can ever do is to let God open the doors and light the paths for your own journey in the light.

No one else on earth has **your** problems and **your** circumstances. But Christ is big enough to take them all and make them work for you! Out of the most unlikely challenges He can produce the most surprising results. With Him in control, you may have plenty of difficulties, but He can help handle them all!

If you are straight and you are determined to *stay* straight and clean, you'll find that you are often tempted and criticized, even persecuted. You'll always be under pressure to give in here, to compromise there, to be like others who walk a low road instead of the high road with Jesus. You may have a tough time of it.

18

The Love Explosion

While I was speaking in a beautiful southern city, I came across a newspaper article on venereal disease, which today has become a fast-growing epidemic. The article mentioned a woman with VD who had been intimate with six different men. Those six had sexual contact with eleven other women. Three of the eleven had relationships with nine other men. So all together this one woman infected with VD was spreading the disease to twenty-six other people.

You could call that a "love explosion," but that would be cheapening the word *love.* So let me tell you about the real love explosion that is happening everywhere today.

Suppose you tried your hardest to reach just one person in the next week with the Good News of Jesus' love. That wouldn't be impossible, would it, if you really worked and prayed to bring that person to Jesus? Suppose you succeeded so well that the new Christian brought one more in the following week, and each new convert brought one more each week. At the end of the second week, there would be four of you in love with Jesus. The third week there would be eight, the fourth week sixteen—the number would double every week, and in ten weeks there would be over a thousand new Christians. By the twentieth week, over a million! It may sound impossible, but it could happen. In fact, it is happening!

A lot of people today are wondering why the Jesus People are multiplying so fast. There's your answer. *It takes just one man or woman, boy or girl who loves the Lord to produce a spiritual explosion to shake the earth.*

At the beginning of this century some zealous Christians had the slogan, "Evangelize the world in this generation and bring back the King!" Since they didn't do it, some people got discouraged and said it could not be done. *It can, and it's happening. Get on the bandwagon!*

Let me tell you how I saw God working in a community I'm going to call Elm City. It began in disappointment. I had been looking forward to holding a series of meetings in another city in May of that year. The meetings were cancelled—just like that. "They didn't give any reason at all," my secretary, Jeanie Weyant, told me. "They just said that circumstances beyond their control made it necessary to withdraw their invitation."

It was hard to understand. I knew some of the unbearable problems in that city, and I had hoped that by speaking there I could be used by the Spirit of God to drive at least the tip of a wedge into that mess of corruption, to give Him a fighting chance. With all its crimes and problems, a city is a strategic center; win a place in it for Christ and you can mold a large part of a nation. So I was deeply disappointed when the cancellation came. But I have learned that God always has a plan better than you can imagine, and I felt a deep peace despite the change.

Meanwhile (as I learned later), in another state, a woman of whom I had never heard felt a strange urgency to pray for her nephew. I will call her Mary Dugan. As Mary later told her nephew, although she could not explain it, she found no rest until she went into her bedroom and poured out from her heart a prayer that God would use her nephew in a special way.

The following morning about ten o'clock Mrs. Dugan was with a group of women in a neighborhood Bible-study class. Again she felt the inexplicable burden of prayer, and she asked the women to join her in prayer for her nephew.

That morning her nephew John Barker was at his desk in the insurance company of which he is president. John is an executive who gives tremendous efforts to his growing business, but that morning he was not thinking of business.

A strange vision came before his eyes. Elm City, where he lives and works, is a historic city of about a hundred thousand people. A year before, a beautiful new civic center had been built there. John had never been inside the million-dollar coliseum, but now he saw it in his mind's eye—filled with people.

They overflowed the oval amphitheatre and stood in the aisles. They were listening to stirring music and forceful preaching of the Gospel. At the invitation, crowds came from all over the vast arena to form a great swelling throng waiting to receive Christ into their lives and hearts.

John Barker had been concerned for some time about Elm City's inability to handle a steadily growing increase in drug addiction, sexual promiscuity, venereal disease, and general deterioration and corruption. A teen-ager in John's own well-to-do neighborhood, Bill Robertson, had wandered down the street only the week before, looking dazed and disoriented. John learned from his own son that Bill was going around with a group of young people rumored to use both marijuana and speed.

Unknown to John Barker, on the day of his waking vision, three boys at the Elm City High School were talking about Bill Robertson. "He's going downhill fast," said one boy.

"Yeah," said another, "but what can you do? He won't listen to anyone."

The third boy said, "We could pray."

And they did—the two boys who happened to be Christians, that is. Not with any fanfare, and usually silently, they asked God to do something to help their friend.

John Barker shared his vision with some other Christian businessmen. They talked and prayed and checked schedules. The next day John called my office.

"I've never done anything like this before," he said, "but some of us in Elm City believe you should come here to hold some evangelistic services. We are ready to rent our civic center this spring, on faith alone—believing that it will be filled and the expenses will be met if you can come."

I explained that most of my meetings are booked far in advance, and that my spring schedule had been completed some time ago. I was honored at the invitation, and I hoped Mr. Barker would understand.

"Nicky," said John Barker, "we were hoping you could come the one spring weekend there is an opening at our coliseum—May sixth and seventh."

Those two days were the ones that had just been cancelled from my engagement calendar.

I accepted. During the next few weeks, while I was crisscrossing the country on other speaking missions, John Barker and his friends were putting their money and their hearts and hands and mouths where their faith was.

They signed a contract for the rental of the Elm City Coliseum for May sixth and seventh.

They put posters all over Elm City: NICKY CRUZ IS COMING.

They got thousands of dollars worth of free time on radio and television in their area, filling it with spot announcements, interviews, and all kinds of publicity about the upcoming crusade. They arranged for the showing of the videotape *No Need to Hide* on May second, the Tuesday evening before my first crusade meeting. In that TV special, Art Linkletter takes me back to my old haunts and we talk about my life and work; as a videotape and a film it has been shown thousands of times.

Plans were made to distribute thousands of copies of my life story—both the original book and a dramatization in comic book form—in all the schools within a hundred miles of Elm City.

They invited the local ministers' association to help with the crusade; especially, they sought the pastors' help in counseling and in telling their congregations about the meetings.

They ran into heavy trouble. The ministers' association voted not to support the crusade. Many of the schools in the area refused to permit the distribution of my books to the students. On May second FBI Director J. Edgar Hoover died, and the whole hour that had been reserved for the showing of *No Need to Hide* was used instead for a memorial tribute to Director Hoover.

John and his friends prayed as soon as the first roadblock appeared, and they kept praying as new ones developed. *Other things began happening.*

A black boy had an argument with a white boy in one of the public schools where distribution of my book had been banned. Another black boy came to the first youngster's aid, two white youths jumped in, and in minutes there emerged what looked like the beginning of a race riot. That week the school board rescinded its ban on *Run Baby Run.*

Word came from another school that there was no objection to distribution of my book on a one-to-one basis. John's friends took stacks of the books home, and Christian young people in the school presented copies personally to everyone who wanted a copy.

In a third school the superintendent telephoned to say that he himself would see that the books were distributed. He did—hundreds of copies.

While the ministerial association never reversed its vote, individual ministers began calling John Barker to say they would participate personally in the crusade. Then they and many of their church members came to classes to learn how to present Christ personally to anyone who would come forward at the evangelistic crusade.

The director of the local TV station moved *No Need to Hide* to the hour that normally carried "Hawaii Five—O."

"We couldn't have hoped for a better time," John's friend Joseph Giles exulted as he told me the story later. "More people watch 'Hawaii Five—O' than any other program!"

When I arrived on Saturday at the Elm City airport, John was there with two of his business friends to drive me to the motel where they had made reservations for me. At lunch they reviewed what they had done, and afterward we went to the civic center to look things over.

Ed Jones, one of John's co-workers, stood beside me as I

looked over the vast coliseum from the speaker's platform. "It holds about eleven thousand people," Ed said. "We have done everything in our power to fill these seats. A group of us walked off the area, section by section, and we claimed every section of it for Jesus Christ. Now it is up to God."

I checked the microphone and the lighting system. As I looked out over the vast arena, it came to me that the portable seats in the center section were too close to the platform. What if God took these humble men at their word, as they had taken Him at His, and sent a multitude of inquirers forward that night to find their Saviour? There was space there for perhaps four hundred seekers. What if the Spirit of God doubled that number?

"Those first three rows of seats," I said, "please take them all out."

A workman asked if the seats could be put lengthwise down the sides of the building, and of course that was fine.

One of the best music groups I know met me in Elm City. I first came across the Singing McCrarys in a church in Los Angeles, and now I have them at my crusades whenever someone like Pat Boone hasn't signed them up first.

Alfred McCrary plays a vibrant bass guitar. Howard McCrary plays the piano. Sometimes Howard plays the piano with one hand and a keyboard instrument called the clavinet with the other, adding a very bouncy effect to the group's singing. Sam McCrary sings with his brothers and their lovely sisters, Linda and Charity.

The McCrarys are young, they are alive, they are with it, and the radiance of the glory of God shines from their faces when they are on a platform. They were in Elm City for a week before I arrived, singing and playing in the schools and churches and helping prepare for the crusade.

That first night of the crusade, the coliseum was filled with thousands of people—especially young people—as the McCrarys started to sing. They did "Let It Be" and other popular numbers. Then they swung into "Rock of Ages" and other familiar hymns.

When they got to "How Great Thou Art," eight thousand people stood up to sing with them, clapping their hands and tapping their feet to the powerful melody, and the music seemed to soar right up to "seventh heaven."

As I waited to speak, I looked at the sea of faces stretching away before me. Busloads had come in from all the surrounding areas, and the parking lot outside was jammed with cars. There were plainly-dressed country people in the audience, men and women who looked well-to-do, and cripples in wheelchairs. They were black and white, young and old. In one section lounged a group of hippies. Teen-agers were everywhere, as well as children of all ages. I thought of the problems and needs of all these people, and as always at such a time I asked God for the words to make Jesus Christ real to them.

I told them what Jesus meant to the streetwalker taken in the act of adultery, and to the hippie usually known as the prodigal son. I spoke of what He means to prodigal sons and daughters I have met myself—runaways, drug addicts, the whole lost generation of this age. I testified to what Jesus means to me.

I said, "I don't care how you look. You can look like Tarzan if you want. You can walk like Jane, you can smell like Cheetah, but Jesus loves you."

This is the big message I always try to make the heart and center of what I say—the love of Jesus. I know how great it is in my own life, and how much He can mean to anyone. I tried to show how beautiful Jesus is.

At the end I asked those who were willing to make a stand for Jesus Christ to stand up and be counted. I do *not* ask for "every head bowed, every eye closed," when I make an appeal for decisions. Deciding for Christ takes courage, and I don't want those I bring to Him to start off ashamed to let people see what they're doing. So I asked those who had decided, to stand and come forward.

At first no one moved. Then a boy who looked about twelve came across the open space to the platform where I stood. That started it. From then on there were lines of people winding down the sides of the amphitheatre, all over that great building, making their stand, coming to find Reality. The McCrarys led in the singing of "Just as I am, without one plea," and as long as the singing went on, those lines continued to surge forward. At last the whole space at the front of the stadium was filled, and people were backed up the aisles.

There were teen-agers, boys and girls, men and women. One young lady had mascara running down her cheeks. I saw a number of youngsters hugging each other in joy. Men and women wiped their eyes and blew their noses.

One young fellow stood by himself, solitary among the seekers, his blond curly hair cascading to his shoulders. I learned later that he was Bill Robertson.

Personal workers, trained for exactly this occasion, led the seekers to counseling rooms—but they overflowed these rooms, and all over the platform small groups talked and prayed together, going through the four spiritual laws outlined by Campus Crusade for Christ. As decisions were witnessed and sealed in prayer, tears gave way to laughter and heavenlike joy. Young people embraced in spiritual ecstasy. For two hours the counseling and rejoicing continued while many crowded around me to shake my hand, to ask questions, to request prayer for loved ones.

When I thought of what this was going to mean in the lives of those who crowded around me, I too found myself close to both tears and great joy. Some of these young people had already started down the horrible trail of carnal indulgence, drug addiction, lawlessness; now they had taken a fork in the road onto higher ground. Some were at a crossroads, and they had turned toward Jesus instead of the devil. What wonderful things God had wrought!

Mary Dugan was in the audience that night, watching the fruit of her prayer. John Barker sat on the platform as chairman of the crusade. After it was all over he said, "It has all happened just as I saw it at my desk three months ago."

One of the Christian businessmen said: "Elm City hasn't had anything like this since Billy Sunday held an evangelistic campaign here. We've been living too long in the past. It's time we let the Spirit of God move us into His program for the twentieth century."

At the final rally of our crusade, the Sunday afternoon of May seventh, thousands again filled the coliseum and hundreds came forward for more decisions for Christ. Before I left Elm City, John Barker and his friends were making plans for the opening of a Nicky Cruz Outreach Center there. With men like that, and with God's Spirit moving as He is today, what an explosion of love can reach out to every man and woman and young person on this planet!

As I said earlier, the real corruptors are the things within us —our inmost attitudes and desires. Only one thing can clean up the spring of corruption in everyone's heart, as I discovered through David Wilkerson years ago. That's why every piece of mail that goes out of my headquarters in Raleigh, North Carolina, is stamped with the words: REMEMBER, JESUS LOVES YOU!

Let me add God's own message about this from the *Living Bible* paraphrase of Romans 13:8–10.

Pay all your debts except the debt of love for others— never finish paying that! For if you love them, you will be paying all of God's laws, fulfilling all His requirements. If you love your neighbor as much as you love yourself you will not want to harm or cheat him, or kill him or steal from him. And you won't sin with his wife or want what is his, or do anything else the Ten Commandments say are wrong. All ten are wrapped up in this one, to love your neighbor as you love yourself. Love does no wrong to anyone. That's why it fully satisfies all of God's requirements. It is the only law you need.

Yes, my friend, whoever you are, wherever you may be when you read this: Remember—Jesus loves *you!*

19

When God Breaks Through

Some time has elapsed since the events of the last chapter. But this book would not be complete unless I shared some very special experiences with you.

Flashing through my mind, many things have bothered me about my ministry. It started out slowly, steadily, and spontaneously, but with the pressures of success seems to have taken on a more mechanical nature.

I can see many ministers, evangelists, and other Christians going through such heavy trials that they do not feel the Lord in their life, and the only thing to hold on to is faith in Christ. Through many dark personal experiences, I found myself thinking that somehow God was trying to change my ministry. I was functioning like a personality and fighting deep down to be just a person. Many times I was fighting because of a young staff with lots of problems. Some young people have been sharp and smart but could not handle pressures in the ministry. I opened my organization to them, but I felt some of them used this ministry to develop their own ministry. That hurt me very much. The Bible tells us "For where your treasure is, there will your heart be also" (Matthew 6:21).

I'm an evangelist, a minister, not an administrator. I know the calling of the Lord. He wants me to present the Gospel. I have seen Him perform many miracles and change lives of many, and now it seems like things are getting a little sour. I traveled so much in 1973—more than 300,000 miles. I began to drift away from many of the things that I should have been on top of. I didn't see Gloria or the children very much. I know this was hard on them. We were drifting further and further apart. I began to distrust people, did not know who my friends were nor whom I could trust. I was aware that evangelists go through pressures of gossip and unfaithfulness in their own organizations. That hurts. My Board of Directors began to see my pressures and my fatigue. As they tried to relieve the pressures, more was being put on me. It is hard when you have to do something and have to agree with others. God gave us good men, men of integrity and I respect them very much. I went through heavy periods of strain and at one of my last meetings, I was coming up from that type of pressure. I came with enthusiasm for a better organization and to pray for a more mature staff. I had a different feeling in my mind and I had a need that was heavy on my heart and they knew of that need.

Edward Birch, as I'm going to call him, seemed to be throwing cold water over everything I proposed. "All this sounds to me like laying out more money," he said. "Where could we find any more than we've already obtained for administrative purposes?" As Director Birch went on, I felt that I was being judged for things that had been beyond my control. There was an apparent harshness in his attitude that made me feel stupid and guilty. It seemed to me that if I was being judged by this man, it was with no compassion at all. I knew Mr. Birch liked to run a tight business, but I wasn't prepared for the apparent fury of his attack on my proposal. I try never to hate anyone, yet a feeling close to hatred and bitterness came over me as he spoke. Eventually my board gave me all the backing I could ask, but at the end of that meeting I felt as depressed and lifeless as a zombie. It was a feeling like trying to fly across the country with no airplane.

I was supposed to leave immediately after the Directors' meeting for a three-day crusade in Canada, but I made up my mind not to go. I felt so depressed. I didn't want to go anywhere. I drove straight home and told Gloria I wasn't going to Canada, dropping my arms down beside me in disgust. "I can't do it," I said. "I just don't feel like going anywhere right now."

Gloria was silent for a moment. Then she said, "Nicky, there will be people in Ottawa waiting to hear you. They have nothing to do with how you feel."

That did it. I knew that Gloria was right, that I couldn't back out of a scheduled crusade just because I was feeling low. By now I had only five mintues to get ready! I called Eastern Airlines and they held my plane for at least twenty minutes until I got aboard. (Right here I want to express my appreciation to Eastern, to Delta Airlines, and to other airlines that have gone out of their way to help me so many times.)

During my engagement in Ottawa I felt completely uninspired. No one at the crusade realized how I was suffering as I spoke; they saw me smiling, but I was only performing. I knew how to perform. I watched the people at the crusade enjoying it all, and I felt like an actor playing a part. After the altar call I felt as though I was putting my hands on empty heads, because I knew my heart wasn't in it. If anyone had known what was really going on he would have knelt down and prayed for Nicky.

Rick Johnson, one of my dedicated fellow workers from the Outreach staff in Raleigh, came with me on this Canada crusade. One of the fine Christians in Ottawa took us both to our hotel, where we checked in at about 2:15 in the morning. We had to get up at 6:00 A.M. to catch a 7:30 plane to Toronto, so I called the hotel operator and asked her to wake me in time. Normally I like to have a hotel room to myself, but I knew Rick was concerned about me so I asked him to stay with me during the few hours before we left. I went to sleep, a very deep sleep.

Sunlight pouring through the hotel windows awakened me at 7:45 the next morning. Turning in disgust to the telephone that should have awakened me earlier, I realized that I had given the operator the room number 1213 instead of the right one—2213. Rick was still sleeping. I woke him and said, "We've missed our plane, Rick. I'm going home." But I found there was no flight with the right connections for some time, so I decided to rest awhile longer and I went back to sleep.

I woke up with tears in my eyes and a tremendous desire to pray, but I felt that I had no power to do it. Rick was asleep. I got on my knees and groaned a prayer without words; something inside me was crying out to God. I felt great pain. I am not a new Christian. I have been growing in the Lord for many years. But I felt the kind of first-love yearning for Christ that a new Christian often feels. My eyes were swollen and red with my emotion and my chest hurt. My body was not ready for such a strong presence of God. He let me know He was there. The whole room glowed with the presence of Jesus. Jesus was like a friend as He sat on the bed next to me. I began talking to Him as I would talk to my wife or my mother. I did not hear a loud voice —there was no need for that. He was there sitting next to me. Never had this happened before. I began to talk to him.

"Jesus, thank You for walking down the streets of New York City, thank You for picking me up with Your strong arms—out of that bondage of sin. Thank You for everything You have done, but Jesus, I'm going through very painful moments now."

Jesus answered, *I know, Nicky.*

I said, "I have done many things wrong, Jesus, and You have helped me through."

I know, Nicky, Jesus said.

"Christians including Dave Wilkerson told me—'Nicky, Jesus loves you.' Even in the Bible You tell me that You loved me first. I have been walking with You, Jesus, for fifteen years and it is now August 1973, and until now, I never knew how much I loved You. I love You Jesus, I love You now, not that You love me, but because I love You. I tell You, I love You, I love You, I love You, I love You."

I began to express my feelings to Him, "Lord Jesus, I have bitterness and hate in my heart and it will destroy me. You are the Great Physician, Lord, and I beg You Lord, with Your hands, heal me inside now."

He told me, *Yes, Nicky, I will do that.*

I felt like I was sleeping, my body felt new, I felt like singing. I was so blessed by God as He took all that hatred away. I did not have that feeling anymore. I began to pray for my wife and my children. Jesus told me that He was going to make me cancel all my crusades so that I could take care of myself and my family.

I said "Jesus, many of these things, I did not ask You to do, but, thank You Lord, for all these blessings." I began to talk to Him about my staff. There had been too much misrepresentation of the whole situation. Pride had possessed many of them. I said, "Lord, if You want them to be removed, do it, but bring more people who can deal with heavy situations."

He said, *I will do it, Nicky.*

I said, "Lord, if anything displeases You, put a stop to it, anything, Lord, any misuse of money in the office or home. Be the guest of my office and my home all the time. Heal the sickness of many souls. Take this nightmare of darkness and terror and these tormenting events of doubt. Take this feeling of insecurity out of my mind."

He replied, *I will do it, Nicky.*

I was still pouring my heart out to Jesus as I confessed to Him my calling. I said, "Lord, You called me into Your ministry. You made it grow. You've given me so much, and I'm thankful. Now please take over once again. You have the wisdom that I don't have. Show me what to do next. You are Love. You are Light. Help me to have the love and the light I need. Help me to grow in the Spirit. Give me Your blessing, Lord, and make me a blessing to everyone I meet. Show me Your glory."

I asked Him to bless Gloria and my little girls. Gloria was pregnant at this time and I asked Him to give us a beautiful baby, the last one, a beautiful, healthy baby. I forgot to ask Him for a boy and we have a beautiful baby girl, Elena Mia. I prayed for my entire family, my supporters, my Board of Directors and I prayed for Mr. Birch. I asked God to take out of my heart every bit of wrong resentment that might be there toward him or anyone else.

I asked the Lord to take care of my ministry and He said He was going to change it. He said: *I want you to trust Me and when*

I finish you are going to see My Glory. I can do all things. I control you, you do not control Me. I will heal the sicknesses of the soul, mind, and body. I have resources of power to fill the restless heart with My Holy Spirit. I told Him about this book. He told me to throw away the first eight chapters and rewrite it. (This I have now done.) He said, *I will bless this book abundantly.* I said, "Thank You, Jesus."

I asked Him to give me grace about pressure in crowds, to help me function as a person and not a personality. I asked Him to give me happiness and He did. I asked Him to take care of the Centers, the financial situation, and all the changes taking place in our organization, and He did.

Wonderful things began happening as I called out to the Lord from my knees. I began to have the strongest feeling of the warmth of His loving presence. Light seemed to be filling the room—light not from this earth, but from clear beyond it.

I began to see things I had never realized before. Things clicked into place in my mind. A memory came back to me from my childhood in Puerto Rico. While I was a small boy there was often a flock of chickens in my parents' backyard. One day I noticed that when the rooster got mad, he was likely to stab out with his beak at whatever chicken was closest. But with the hens it was different. One hen ruled the roost when the rooster wasn't around. This hen pecked at another one when she was angry, and that one would peck at still another, and so it went down the line. There was a thin, scraggly little chicken at the bottom of the heap that always got it last of all. She was a sad sight; there wasn't anyone else she could peck at.

I realized that I had been caught in a sort of pecking order, too. Smarting from hurt feelings, I'd been taking my feelings out on those "below" me. I promised God that with His help I wouldn't do that again.

While I was praying and meditating, Rick woke up and felt the presence of the Lord. He couldn't believe it. He began receiving such a blessing that he was crying, and he began to pray with a beautiful spirit of compassion and humility and dedication. I prayed, too, but now it was mostly praise and thanksgiving for God's infinite love and all His promises and power and guidance. I thanked Him for Rick and for all the many people who make the Outreach possible. And as I prayed, love filled my heart for each person I named, including Mr. Birch. I suddenly felt very thankful for that man's financial wisdom and his concern for keeping our Outreach ministry sound and solvent.

I looked at my watch. I had spent almost three and one-half hours with Jesus in person. What a great joy, what a great thrill! He really healed me. Jesus really healed me.

I knew something was happening to me that I had never felt before. The promise of the Twenty-third Psalm came into my mind:

The Lord is my shepherd; I shall not want.
He maketh me to lie down in green pastures:
  he leadeth me beside the still waters.
He restoreth my soul . . . .
I will fear no evil: for thou art with me . . . .
  my cup runneth over.
Surely goodness and mercy shall follow me all the days of
  my life: and I will dwell in the house of the Lord for ever.

And I remembered Jesus' parable of the shepherd with a hundred sheep (*see* Matthew 18:12–14). When one of the sheep got lost, the shepherd left the other ninety-nine sheep behind and looked everywhere until he found the lost one and brought it safely home. From my study in Bible college I knew how a shepherd in the Holy Land would take care of a lost lamb. He would hold the little lamb close to his chest for two weeks. The lamb comes to love the warmth and tenderness of the shepherd's body. The shepherd would hold the lamb and look after it and feed it all through the day and sleep with it through the night. Finally he would let the lamb go, but it would have learned its lesson: it would never leave the shepherd more than a few feet away.

Some words came back to me from a wise old teacher in Bible college:

In the Holy Land, when a lamb strays like that, sometimes the shepherd breaks the lamb's leg. Then he carefully sets the broken limb and keeps it in splints and bandages. He carries it tenderly in his arms and lets the lamb get used to the warmth and even his heartbeat. He cares for it this way until it is completely healed and strong again. He does it in love, to teach the lamb a very important lesson—and to save its life.

As I thought of all this, I made a startling discovery.

THE SHEPHERD HAD JUST BROKEN ME.

I realized that Jesus had broken my pride, my roughness, my bad thoughts, my defensiveness. He had been rebuking me, and He had healed me. There was oil for my wounds, heavenly balm for my bruises. I felt His loving arms holding me. And I felt the beauty of His holiness and purity.

It's hard to put this into words, but at the same time I felt how important it is to take a clear-cut stand for the Lord. I saw how foolish it is to compromise your Christian testimony or fool around with anything wrong. I felt the truth of the message:

. . . God is light, and in him is no darkness at all.

If we say that we have fellowship with him, and walk in darkness, we lie, and do not the truth:

But if we walk in the light, as he is in the light, we have fellowship one with another, and the blood of Jesus Christ his Son cleanseth us from all sin.

If we say that we have no sin, we deceive ourselves, and the truth is not in us.

If we confess our sins, he is faithful and just to forgive us our sins, and to cleanse us from all unrighteousness.

1 John 1:5–9

Cleanse us from all unrighteousness! That's what God wants us to do. To make His children spiritually strong and whole, free from corruption of any kind. To use us to bring His other children Home.

As all this came to me in that hotel room, there was such a time of praise! I wish I could share it with you, but some things just cannot be put into human language.

Let me just say this, though: Jesus was there in that hotel room, and I knew it and Rick knew it. The glory of those hours is with me now, and will stay with me.

Now I know how Moses felt when he took off his shoes at the burning bush. I left Ottawa with a new vision of holiness unto the Lord. I feel more deeply than ever before how vital it is to be completely dedicated if you want to do the Lord's work. I have a new passion now, to make every word count. One day I'll be passing on from earth to heaven, and I want to be sure that my work and my words will go on for the Lord.

After we returned to Raleigh, Rick and I shared some of our experiences at our staff prayer meeting. Rick's wife, Sarah, who was also on our staff at the time (right now she's looking after a new baby), told us: "You know, while you two were in Ottawa, I was praying and I felt the same burden for complete consecration."

It's a long way from corruption to consecration—like the distance between darkness and light, or sickness and health, or death and life. The one is the complete opposite of the other. Yes, the one is the *only* answer to the other.

No sensible person would choose sickness instead of health, or death instead of life. Then why do the *corruptors* have such a hold on the world? Maybe because the people trapped by them don't know what glorious freedom they could have in Jesus.

And anyone who finds how great He is, drops the corrupting things the way a young man leaves the toys behind, when he grows up, and turns to the things of manhood and reality.

But so many people are still playing with things that aren't important at all. As I think of the years ahead, I see unbelievable changes taking place all over the world. I am convinced that the foundations of our faith, our homes, and our society will be shaken as never before. Many things that are precious to us will almost disappear from sight.

There may be less drug addiction in the next few years. However, although we have become more educated about drugs, we will still have to live with it. There will also be an incredible increase in addiction to witchcraft, spiritualism, Satanism, Eastern religions and false gods, although more ministers are getting together to fight the occult, and the blood of Christ will be applied to every Christian. There will be a veneer of peace in the world, but underneath there will be more spiritual conflict and anguish than ever before. There will be widespread revolt against every form of moral restraint.

Some people think the pendulum will swing back soon toward the way things used to be. *I don't.* I see ahead of us more sensuality, more nudity, more sexual perversion, more open attacks on the home and the family and God and the church and government. I believe it's going to become harder and harder to be faithful to Jesus Christ. I see evil becoming so attractive that many are deceived and corrupted. I believe TV and movies will bring about this corruption. I see the powers of the demonic world openly displayed and applauded. In these last days there will be more divorces than ever before. Satan is going to be attacking Christian marriages more and more.

Ahead of us there is chaos and revolution. Problems that our physicians and psychiatrists thought they had under control will become too much for them. Shortages and inflation will increase until only the few will be able to buy what they want. A depression will sweep over the whole civilized world.

The people of God will be tested as never before. This is not a vision nor a prophecy but the experience of traveling and being sensitive to our environment and this world, and I believe that many educators and ministers feel as I do.

I personally feel that there will be a tremendous love between

Catholics and Protestants in these last days in the name of Jesus. I believe they will all sit down together at the "banquet table" singing and praising the Lord, shouting *Hosanna* to Jesus Christ, the Son of the Everlasting God.

BUT JESUS LIVES! HE AND THE HOLY SPIRIT WILL GIVE STRENGTH AND BLESSING TO EVERYONE WHO FOLLOWS HIM. PRAISE HIS NAME!

If you would like more information about our work, write to: Nicky Cruz Outreach, Box 27706, Raleigh, North Carolina 27611.

Postscript

At 5:40 this afternoon, April 30, 1974, I put the last touch on this book. I now have the most beautiful staff, just as God promised me. He has sent me fellow workers as talented as they are dedicated. Jim DeVries, employed for twelve years by Sarns, Inc. in Michigan as production manager, is my executive director. LaRue Price is my personal secretary. She holds prayer meetings for our staff in the office and has opened the Outreach offices to the public. People call in constantly for prayer and we pray with them over the telephone. I was deeply touched recently when I talked personally with a lady who phoned in long distance. This woman had been trying to reach me for several days while I was away ministering in a crusade. She told me that she was a hustler and had syphilis. We prayed together over the telephone and we were so broken by the Lord that we both began to cry. Some days later I got a letter from this lady testifying that she had accepted Christ and had been proven completely healed by her physician. She wrote that her husband, with whom she had been having so many problems, had also found Christ and that they now have a very beautiful marriage. These are just a few of the blessings that I had been missing.

When God breaks through I become very happy, and He has broken through, my friend—I **LOVE YOU.**

Your friend and servant,
Nicky Cruz